Chaldean Numerology and Predictive Astrology

A Guide to Divination, Numbers, and the Zodiac

Your Free Gift
(only available for a limited time)

Thanks for getting this book! If you want to learn more about various spirituality topics, then join Mari Silva's community and get a free guided meditation MP3 for awakening your third eye. This guided meditation mp3 is designed to open and strengthen ones third eye so you can experience a higher state of consciousness. Simply visit the link below the image to get started.

https://spiritualityspot.com/meditation

Table of Contents

Part 1: Chaldean Numerology

Unlock Ancient Secrets Surrounding Numbers, Divination, and Astrology

Introduction

Numerology is a fascinating method of divination, and it holds so many treasures for those who dive deep into it. And you better believe it when I say it's the golden goose that continues laying egg after egg, each one more valuable than the last.

Numbers are all around us, and they influence every aspect of our lives, whether we know and accept that or not. Those who have chosen to look into the science and energies of numbers have had no reason to look back because they're enjoying the benefits of choosing to live life according to the laid-out plans our souls have for us.

This is something the wise ancients known as the Chaldeans knew, and it's why they developed such a rich, beautiful, and in-depth system of numbers that allows everyone, young and old, rich or poor, to have a shot at self-actualization.

The thing about following what your soul has set forth for you is that you'll eventually find your life full of love, laughter, joy, and true fulfillment. You'll no longer feel the desire to continue chasing the next big thing, the next higher high, the next better, bigger thing. You'll finally be able to step off that hamster wheel and just breathe because you're embodying everything you were supposed to be and then some.

This book is one of the best ones out there because you won't find yourself confused about what the terms mean or how you're supposed to do the math on the numbers that affect your life. You'll find that it goes straight to the point, and it contains a great deal of information to start you off on your journey with numbers.

If you're ready to change your life for the better and take things to the next level, you're in for a treat. Buckle up, and let's get started.

Chapter 1: Introduction to Chaldean Numerology

Who Were the Chaldeans?

Close to the rivers Tigris and Euphrates, a special group of people called the Chaldeans (pronounced as kal-day-ans) crafted a very interesting form of numerology that is ridiculously accurate when it comes to describing people's traits and lives. The people were the Chaldeans of Babylonia. It's not quite clear where they came from, but somehow, they were able to take over the throne of Babylon. You may have heard of Nebuchadnezzar. He was just one of their many kings, and the people dwelled in the land for the better part of at least 75 years.

The Chaldean's lived by the River Tigris.

So, what's so special about them? After all, there was already basic infrastructure available at the time for them to live their lives as they took over from the original occupants of the land. Well, they did come in with very advanced innovations in the fields of mathematics and astrology. Not only that, but they also had some more refined views on matters of spirituality at the time, introducing elements such as divination, magic, and the worship of the moon by recognizing her undeniable effect on humanity.

However, all their achievements and their faith are still confounding as they didn't do much by way of recording them, and it's a wonder how they were able to spread their influence and ideas all over the West. We may have lost access to all the other things they knew, but thank goodness what they knew as numerology is around for us to work with today. Why? Because out of all the other forms of numerology, this one is scarily accurate.

Introduction to Chaldean Numerology

Chaldean numerology is centered on the idea that all is energy. Everything vibrates at its own unique frequency, and some frequencies work better with certain ones than with others. So, all the letters of the alphabet and the numbers and sounds have their unique vibrations, which you can use to extrapolate a lot of information about your life path and other things you may have been in the dark on. You're about to discover a world of wonder.

The thing about this version of numerology is that it was the first to put together the actual vibratory interpretations of each letter. It developed a detailed analysis of one's name, tying that in with the date of birth by looking at each number's specific frequency so that you can figure out the truth about who you are and why you're here. Sadly, many people assume this is a difficult form of numerology and divination because that couldn't be further from the truth. You can learn this, and you'll be glad you did by the time you're done with this book because you'll never feel like you're lost and flailing around in life anymore.

Vibrations and Frequencies

Again, all things are made up of energy, expressing themselves differently. You have a unique vibration or "vibe" of your own, one that is distinctly identifiable by everyone around you. Scientifically speaking, your vibration is the unique way in which your energy oscillates, while frequency is the rate of that oscillation, whether fast or slow. So, when it comes to Chaldean numerology, the goal is to find out exactly what sort of vibration you've got and how that presents in the world by way of the frequencies you put out through sound, numbers, and letters. Everything is energy, everything vibrates, and everything has a signature frequency that has a very real effect on everything and everyone around it.

So, when it comes to your personal vibe, the best way to pinpoint that would be to work with your name, which has a lot of clues about the way you think, your power, how you conduct yourself, and so much more. So, let's think again about the idea of vibrations when it comes to, say, music. You listen to a song played on a guitar, and you can pick up on a few specific notes played at varying levels of intensity and some chords that are a combo of notes played together. However, they have different rates of vibration; their frequencies mesh well together because if they didn't, they wouldn't create a harmonious sound. Another interesting thing about these notes is that they have resonance. For instance, if you strike a G note on a guitar and there's another guitar in the room, a fascinating thing happens — the other guitar's G note will be affected as well.

Chaldean numerology shows us that you can't just take them at face value when it comes to names. You have to break them down into component parts because every letter in the alphabet has its own unique background, history, and meaning. You can learn about your life path, where you're likely to excel, what you struggle with, your patterns of behavior, and the things you're likely to have issues with spiritually speaking. No other numerology system does this better than the Chaldean one.

A, B, C, D...

Let's talk about the alphabet. What we have right now in English is the furthest thing from what the Chaldeans worked with back in their day. Instead, they used cuneiform, a set of interesting-looking symbols that were absolutely necessary for the survival and thriving of their culture. They would write this cuneiform on clay tablets that they'd wet and dry out. Their cuneiform looked the way it did because it was much easier to write straight lines on the wet clay. Trying to write the letter B or C would have been problematic. So, this begs the question, if they used an entirely different set of symbols than we do, how could we possibly work with

Chaldean numerology at all?

Here's your answer. The thing is that the symbols and sounds that they worked with were integrated and adapted to suit other writing systems such as the Egyptian hieroglyphics and other additions from the Romans, Hebrews, Phoenicians, and Greeks. However, through all of these changes, the essential meanings from Chaldean numerology stuck around for several thousands of years. Remember, this system of numerology emphasizes the importance of sound and its meaning, and no matter how you represent the sound "ah" in written form, for instance, it will always be the same sound.

This form of numerology is so good that even though our alphabet is different from cuneiform, we can still accurately glean the meaning of all the words we say without figuring out how to write in an ancient language.

The Thing about Letters and Numbers...

Let's talk about yin and yang for a second. It's the concept that there's good, and there's bad, and there's bad in the good and good in the bad. In the same way, letters and numbers can have both positive and negative meanings. It's not bad that there are positive and negative vibrations for each letter and number. It's a good thing because when you learn what you're struggling with, you can simply look for the flip side, which will show you what you need to do to fix things.

When it comes to this system of numerology, you need to keep in mind that the more powerful the number, the riskier the negative aspects can be for you. So, the more positive potential a number carries, the more you need to be wary of its corresponding negative potential.

Comparing Chaldean Numerology to Pythagorean Numerology

You might be aware of other popular types of numerology, like Pythagorean numerology. This was crafted by Pythagoras himself sometime around 500 BCE. There are major differences between these two forms of numerology, so it is important not to get them mixed up if you've already studied Pythagoras' version.

First of all, Chaldean numerology doesn't work with the number 9 because this number is reverently seen as being divine, and so out of respect for divinity, they didn't include it on their chart. However, it was fine for the number to be used as part of the total of a name or word; it just wasn't ascribed to any specific letter. The Pythagorean system works with the numbers 1 through 9. For the Chaldeans, 9 is thought of as the number of infinity, and it makes sense why they thought that way. *When you multiply 9 by any number and add the digits in the resulting figure, you'll always get 9.* For instance, 9 multiplied by 3 will give you 27. Add 2 and 7, and you get 9. Here's a more random example: 9 multiplied by 47563 will give you 428,067. Add all the digits in that result, and you'll get 27; 2 plus 7 equals 9. Whip out your calculator and check that out with different numbers, and you'll see for yourself. It's fascinating stuff. However, it appears Pythagoras didn't really care about all that because he assigned the figure to the letters I and R.

Another key difference is that the Pythagorean version has no interest in the unique vibrations each sound produces. As far as Pythagoras was concerned, what was more interesting was just the patterns that lay in the sequence of numbers and nothing more.

One more cool thing that Chaldean numerology has over Pythagorean is that, while the latter is only concerned with your birth name, the former acknowledges that you have the right to change your name and whatever name you're using is valid. It's all about the effect your present name has on you. It doesn't bind you to your name, especially if you never liked it. For the Chaldeans, every change in the name is accounted for because, like it or not, having a new name will mean new vibrations and changes in your life, not just in terms of what people call you but also on an energetic level. Also, of all the systems out there, the Chaldean one is the only one that understands that letters aren't just about numerical values but actually have their own meaning.

Comparing Chaldean Numerology to Kabbalah Numerology

Kabbalah numerology is Hebrew, and it's only about your birth name as well, like the Pythagorean version. Kabbalah is all about knowing one's soul and mind and has nothing to do with things that happen in the physical world. It's more about the mental aspect of life.

Since this form of numerology is rooted in a culture that reveres faith and religious beliefs, you should know that it's rooted in the ideology of God as the creator of all life. Kabbalah holds that God was able to do this by using the Hebrew letters, which have power on their own and their assigned numbers. In fact, those who follow the way of Kabbalah also work with something called *gematria*, which offers a way to interpret various words and find the associated meanings, something that is useful for them when it comes to the interpretation of the Bible.

Kabbalah acknowledges that to make calculations in the form of numerology; there are exactly ten categories of energies that one needs to work with. They are:

1. Kether
2. Chokhmah
3. Binah
4. Chesed
5. Geburah
6. Tiphareth
7. Netzach
8. Hod
9. Yesod
10. Makuth

On the subject of vibrations, Kabbalah acknowledges that there are 22 vibrations spanning a range of 1 through to 400. While this system seems to be all about self-awareness and aspires to reach the highest levels of consciousness, the truth is it doesn't hold a candle to Chaldean numerology because it only works with first and middle names. It doesn't bother with your date of birth, and the only reason it's so popular is that many celebrities are declaring themselves to be followers of Kabbalah.

Tamil Numerology

Tamil numerology is also known as Vedic or Indian numerology and is an ancient form of this divination system. It also works with the numbers 1 to 9, like the Pythagorean system. There are three important numbers in this system:

- The psychic number
- The destiny number
- The name number

These numbers are very important because they help you identify your innate qualities, including the things you may not have realized about yourself yet. It also helps with predicting the future, but that's about it.

Why You Should Choose Chaldean Numerology Instead

Chaldean numerology has a lot of benefits that other numerology systems lack. It is not only the most accurate system in terms of your life path number, but it also helps you improve your life and learn more about yourself. If you are serious about realizing your destiny, you need to learn how to use this ancient system.

The reason numerology systems have been around for so long is that they help millions of people see the truth about themselves. It helps you understand what is happening in your life and even helps you learn how to better yourself. But not all systems are created equal.

The benefits of having a great life path number are many. I say "a great life path number" because it matters, unlike some other numerology numbers that don't tell you anything about yourself or leave things vague just because they deem them unimportant. This is where Chaldean numerology excels above all other numerology systems. It helps you learn your life path number, how to better yourself, and ultimately figure out the meaning of life and why you're here. The great thing about this system is that it breaks down your entire name, taking into account each letter and the numbers behind them.

It is impossible to improve your life unless you know what needs improvement. Every time we go through a certain experience, good or bad, we make a certain amount of progress. Those experiences help us change for the better, but only when we know what exactly needs changing.

For example, let's say you have a hard time in your career and start to feel like life is not where it should be. Wouldn't it be nice to know that you are supposed to seek more wisdom or knowledge? This is the kind of thing that a Chaldean numerology reading will help you figure out. You should definitely pick up this ancient art to change your life completely and become a better person. You don't want to leave your fate to chance.

Chapter 2: From Numbers to Planets and Back

Astrology and numerology are connected to each other, and in this chapter, you'll learn how the planets relate to each number.

Astrology and numerology are connected.
https://pixabay.com/es/photos/sistema-solar-sol-mercurio-venus-439046/

Number 1 Personality Traits

This number corresponds with the Sun, which is the source of all life and why everything is still in its place. Without the Sun, it's tough to imagine how any form of life can survive. If your birthday falls on the 28th, 19th, or 1st, you're under the influence of this number. The same goes if your name's value is 1.

If you're born under the influence of this number, chances are you're a person who values honesty, and if people had to describe you, they'd say there's a certain dignity about the way you do things. There's a chance you're never caught dressed horribly, and you walk around like you own the place. You have no issues doling it out on anything when it comes to money.

When it comes to working, you always give it everything you've got, and for this reason, success never evades you. You're a straight shooter who doesn't see any sense in dishonesty, and you often call it as you see it. You have no room in your heart to harbor hate, you're not the sort of person to play your cards close to the chest, and you would never consider betraying someone or a cause in a million years. Sadly, not everyone can handle how frank you are, which can earn you a little bit of enmity from others.

No one ever has to guess where they stand with you because they'll know whether you like them or hate them. Also, you're not desperate for anyone's friendship or company; instead, you're a magnet that draws people to you because you're naturally a helpful person, and your honesty is a rare quality that many people seek.

Your mind is sharp, and nothing gets past you, so no one could ever put one over you because you can tell what they're really about. Your sharp mind also allows you to excel at things like mystical sciences, arts, metaphysical matters, music, and all things related to art.

The Sun's Influence on Number 1

You're a hard worker. No one could ever accuse you of being lazy, and you're always doing one thing or another. You're also the furthest thing from covetous, preferring to be happy for others and their accomplishments.

Just as the Sun rules over the entirety of our star system, you're the kind of person who can be found heading things, often nominated to be at the helm of affairs. The sun's influence makes it so you would do very well as a politician or administrator in charge of others. It's not uncommon to find 1's all over the political space.

Number 2 Personality Traits

The number 2 is yin (or a feminine number). Chaldean Numerology symbolizes love, peace, marriage, and partnership. 2 is a perfect balance of masculine and feminine energies. You know that you can always count on someone with a 2 Life Path for support and partnership in any endeavor in life.

If your Life Path number is a 2, then you have great empathy for others and have much love to give to those around you. You'll spend time tending to the needs of an individual before tending to your own if necessary because you possess that characteristic nurturing quality that most people need at some point in their lives. You should try to avoid becoming overly possessive or dependent on another person, and you'll find that your relationships will become more solid and lasting.

The tendency for a 2 is to want to be needed because of the desire to love. You may have been overprotected in childhood by your mother, but this is likely because she is accustomed to being alone and did not have a man around at the time. Many people with a Life Path number of 2 also have histories marked by broken relationships, especially in the case of separation or divorce. They have a thirst for harmony with others and tend to get along well with almost everyone they encounter.

If you are a 2, you can be an ideal companion and friend. You tend to be very loyal and trustworthy unless someone gives you cause not to be. You are willing to take care of almost anyone for as long as necessary because you seek long-lasting union in your relationships. Your favorite type of relationship is one based on friendship because it is more likely to endure over the years. It is important that if a relationship starts out with romance and lust, it is not allowed to continue if the feelings begin to fade away. If you find that you cannot commit for a long time, you may tend to be promiscuous. A relationship is most likely to last if one partner does not take advantage of the other. You can become jealous if someone else dares to flirt with or show interest in your significant other.

2 is usually quiet and prefers not to cause an unnecessary commotion. If they are often on the outside looking in, they want more out of life than they are being given by those around them, which often leads them to struggle with their relationships for years before anything changes for the better. The tendency for someone with a 2 Life Path is to get along well with almost everyone and enjoy the benefits of a long-lasting and solid relationship if they can make it through the trials they go through at the beginning.

The Moon's Influence on Number 2

The Moon covers love, partnership, and compassion. It also represents illusionary thought, or what some would call mind games. The moon influences number 2 people, and you can tell by how emotional they are.

The Moon rules the night. It is the only natural satellite of planet Earth, and its job is to illuminate the dark side of our world. This is where this number gets its attributes; those born on day 2 have a deep connection with the earth and a love for the nighttime and all things it brings. They have a way of being the light in the dark for those going through troubling times.

Number 3 Personality Traits

Number 3 has been described as the number of creativity, imagination, and self-expression. Chaldean numerology uses the number three to represent someone who is expressive and imaginative in their work. Number 3 people are typically very creative in their endeavors, often coming up with new, innovative ideas that set them apart from the crowd.

When it comes to relationships and friendships, these types of people are affectionate and nurturing partners who are happy to take care of others. They tend to be very popular with friends because they behave in a friendly manner that others want to get close to them. This type of number also tends to have many relationships with many people. Number 3 people can be very generous and will happily share their possessions with others. It is up to you to ensure that they know you are open to receiving the gifts.

Those who do have a relationship with the number 3 often tend to take care of others at their own cost. However, it is important for this type of person to occasionally listen to their own needs because sometimes they can get so caught up in helping everyone else that they forget about themselves.

Regarding health and well-being, number 3 people tend toward a generally positive outlook on life. They are seen as creative souls who can make excellent scientists, writers, and poets. Often, they will find themselves surrounded by many friends who are helping them to develop their talents. Due to some of their other characteristics, number 3 people find themselves being very comfortable in work environments that do not focus too heavily on rules and regulations. The more relaxed these environments are, the better these types of people will be at dealing with them.

Number 3 people are also friendly and easy to get along with but tend toward a more mature approach to life than usual. These are often the types of people that others gravitate toward because they have a calming, soothing effect on others. If you have a number 3 friend, you'll find that their relaxed and friendly nature can rub off on you in time.

Number 3's can also be very supportive partners. They often know how to help other people overcome their problems and will be happy to lend any assistance they can for the other person to succeed. The number 3 personality is considered to be very lucky, especially when it comes to their career. This type of person will have plenty of employment opportunities, not necessarily because they are better than anyone else but simply because their natural ability to create new and innovative ways to do things attracts others to them. Their imagination is one of this type's greatest strengths, and it can be used to achieve many great things in the workplace.

Jupiter's Influence on Number 3

Jupiter.
NASA/JPL-Caltech/SwRI/MSSS/Kevin M. Gill, Public domain, via Wikimedia Commons:
https://commons.wikimedia.org/wiki/File:PIA22946-Jupiter-RedSpot-JunoSpacecraft-20190212.jpg

Chaldean numerology assigns this number to Jupiter, the planet of luck, success, and prosperity. These people are very fortunate and enjoy a happy life because of their good fortune.

Jupiter is also an astrological analogy for protective spiritual forces that govern everything we do. Its affinity with the number 3 means that those born under this sign are extremely lucky in all aspects of their lives and always have something good to look forward to. These natives are usually successful in whatever they do.

Number 4 Personality Traits

Number 4 is a number related to security, conservatism, and practicality. It is considered to be the number of the realist. This type of person has difficulty letting go of tradition and outdated ideas. Number 4 people often have difficulty expressing themselves in front of others and can present a very stubborn view of their ideals.

They can often see the bad in everything while ignoring or even discarding the good. This is why they have such a difficult time communicating with others. This type of person also tends toward a negative outlook on the future, always expecting the worst and fearing that they will lose those closest to them. They can be very imaginative and dramatic, often coming up with overly dramatic ways to express themselves.

4's are often good at being practical or from a business perspective. They usually have a very good head for finances and have little difficulty in managing their money. This does not mean that this type of person is selfish. Quite the opposite, in fact, they tend to take care of others financially with great generosity and are there for others when needs arise. They also tend to be very loyal to those they care about and will stand by them no matter what.

It is important to note that those born on the number 4 are often described as being very idealistic. They often have the best of intentions and always want the best for others. However, it is not unknown for them to have their own ideas of what their chosen course should be. Number 4 people can sometimes be too stubborn for their own good and hold onto their ideals for far too long. They can also be very adaptable in situations others would find difficult every now and then. People born under number 4's influence generally know how to bend the rules and regulations to achieve their goals. They are not known for being particularly honest but for finding ways to get what they need. This adaptiveness can make these types of people very useful in the workplace, as they know how to work with others and can smooth over difficult situations.

4's tend toward a certain level of obsessiveness which often accompanies the negative side of this number. This type of person constantly worries and finds things to be displeased about. If a number 4 person cannot let go of some of these concerns, their mind will constantly wander, and they will spend a great deal of time on the daydreaming side.

They can be very good at creating status symbols and are often collectors. They would rather buy something nice for themselves and those around them than actually need it and will often spend far more than they need to on objects they see as having some sort of value, even if these objects may seem like nothing more to others than trash. They have an artistic nature in thought or work and are also very creative in certain areas. They can see things from a different perspective and can often come up with ideas that others may not be able to think of. This type of person is often very good at being a leader and can often take charge of people and situations.

Uranus's Influence on Number 4

The number 4 is characterized by being patient, disciplined, and goal-oriented with a strong need for order in their life. Uranus brings the radical impulse of change to them. For this, they may be thrown off balance by the unexpected things Uranus brings with it, and the clash between their need for order and change can lead to strife in their lives.

There is one remedial action to take in this case: If you're a number 4, practice clearing everything out of your space so that new things don't come into your life or onto your radar too unexpectedly. You may not be able to control the world around you, but you can at least try to control your own space.

Number 5 Personality Traits

Number 5 is the number of pleasure and fascination. This type of person usually has a very wide range of interests. This includes areas such as art, music, playing sports, languages, or even gambling for recreation. These types of people see everything around them as playthings and are quick to see the fun in everything. They enjoy learning new things, and they always seek knowledge.

5's are often very good at making friends and enjoying the company of others. They can be very energetic, share their energy in many different ways, and are often quite sociable. They tend to have problems with understanding others, though, as they seem to have issues understanding the symbolism behind things or being able to tell what others have a problem with.

This type of person is often a bit too easygoing for their own good, as they will tend to go along with most suggestions even if they do not agree with them. They will also not necessarily see the negative aspects of these suggestions and may not be able to see their relevance. This can cause problems when it comes to expressing themselves or even handling criticism.

Number 5 people can often be quite good at keeping up appearances and are often seen as being friendly and sociable. However, this does not always mean that they are happy with their own life but rather that they are good at pretending to be happy. They tend to view life through a certain lens they have created for themselves, one in which everything is a game and people need to treat them the same way. This can cause problems when it comes to being overly negative, as this type of person may be good at hiding their true feelings to keep up appearances.

They are often very creative and enjoy having the opportunity to express themselves and others in different ways. They are very good at improvising and often play with things. They also tend to be rather competitive and can often spend a great deal of time getting ahead of others and proving that they are better than them at something. They love feeling like they have accomplished something no one else has done before or even thought of doing before.

Number 5 personalities are often very helpful in friendships but can also be very jealous. This can cause issues in relationships and may cause problems when it comes to sharing things with others. They generally do not like to share the spotlight, and it can become difficult if others take attention away from them. They can fit into almost any situation or group of people with relative ease. They have an air of security around them, which allows them to get along with many different types of people and helps them with social interactions. They are often quite good at listening to others and understanding their feelings and their issues. 5's tend to be very generous and kind, always willing to help others out whenever they can. This type of person is not easily seen as a bully by anyone and generally has a lot of friends to help them in times of need.

Mercury's Influence on Number 5

Mercury, the planet of communication, is the ruler of number 5. Mercury also has a strong association with intellect and information. Mercury can be generous and provides luck to those in need but can also manipulate consciousness in negative ways. People may feel insecure about who their true friends are. The psychological effects are they may feel like they're not getting what they deserve or that others are taking advantage of them or just not being there for them as much as they would like for them to be. Number 5 would do well to understand that the only one responsible for always showing up for them is themselves.

Number 6 Personality Traits

The number 6 person does not fight as hard for their rights as others and tends to be very relaxed in this area. Their life plans are often rather vague and hard to pin down, but they are not necessarily unwilling to participate in anything important or beneficial in any way.

Number 6 people tend to be very generous with their emotions and can sometimes be very devious when dealing with others. Very often, they will be at odds with the system around them because they feel like these systems do not work properly and that they should be changed in some way. This type of person tends to feel as though they need to make changes in their life as a whole, but they are often not aware of how these changes will affect them personally nor how important these same changes are to other people.

This type of person may also be very good at wrapping things up and wrapping up a conversation or an argument with the right words and phrases. They may even use this ability to get ahead, trying to make it seem like they are less intelligent than they really are and using this to manipulate others. This can cause them problems when it comes time for school or work.

6's are very emotional and rather dramatic, making it difficult for them to fit in or even do well at a certain job or career. This is not to say that they cannot accomplish anything, but rather that they must learn to accept the idea of compromise to achieve their goals or those of someone else. They must look outside themselves and see what other people want before they can work toward achieving their own desires. This will cause some friction with other types of personalities and may even cause problems with those closest to them.

Number 6 people tend to be social and like to be around others. They are usually willing to try new things, go out with others and act a bit silly to make other people happy. However, they tend to get easily bored with things in general and can become very cranky at times. They do not like conflict, and if given a choice between leaving a problem or putting up with it, then they will rarely choose the latter.

When it comes to friendships, number 6 people are usually very honest when dealing with others and able to compromise when necessary. They are generally good at listening hard when someone wants them to listen and accept their opinions. This type of person may also be slightly sneaky and underhanded when it comes to getting what they want.

They can fit into almost any situation or group of people with relative ease. They have an air of security around them, which allows them to get along with many different types of people and helps them with social interactions. They are often quite good at listening to others and understanding their feelings and their issues.

Venus's Influence on Number 6

Venus.
https://commons.wikimedia.org/wiki/File:Venus_globe.jpg

Because of Venus, these people tend to be very friendly and helpful, almost to a fault. They are constantly trying to help others, and helping is their favorite pastime. Many of these individuals are prone to offering unsolicited advice or ideas about problems. Others will take up the causes that their friends believe in, even if they themselves do not share those same beliefs. They would rather "help" than "hurt." The Chaldean Numerology theory shows how Venus always tries to heal whatever ails you. These people truly shine when they can help and care for other people.

Number 7 Personality Traits

7 is a lucky number and a sign of good fortune. This numeral can also be seen as "the seeker" or "the thinker." This personality type manifests as systematic thinkers who rarely change their minds about things. They are excellent managers who don't like getting involved in other people's problems. The 7 personality type has very high moral standards and is discreet – even secretive – when they keep their thoughts to themselves.

They are always honest and trustworthy but do not really like to participate in social activities. They like being alone and are quiet by nature. They are also very private, speaking only when they have something important to say. Integrated individuals with a 7 personality type believe that life is all about balance, values, and principles. They love reading books, solving mathematical problems, and gardening. The best career choices for them include mathematics, engineering, medicine, science, or any other field of research.

People with this personality type tend to be calm yet withdrawn most of the time. They often prefer being alone to mingling with others at gatherings or parties. When they are in a group of people, they do not introduce themselves to other strangers. People with this personality type are very practical and systematic when dealing with problems.

People with the number 7 personality type have strong analytical skills and intense powers of concentration. They can work on a task for long hours without losing focus or getting distracted by other things. They are straightforward and honest people who respect tradition, faith, family, and personal values above everything else. They believe in working hard so that their family can enjoy the fruits of their labor. At the same time, they desire respect instead of popularity.

They are sensual and charming individuals who are very picky about their partners. They always choose partners who can match them intellectually and emotionally. Number 7 people do a lot of traveling within their lifetime because they need to escape the trappings of everyday routine to keep them feeling fresh and energetic. They may hide their true feelings from others, but that does not mean they lack emotions or empathy.

Neptune's Influence on Number 7

As a number 7, you have an air of mystery. It's difficult to know what you are thinking or feeling because your mind is constantly moving. Neptune is like the morning fog that quickly disperses and leaves the world around you refreshed and alive with new ideas and possibilities.

The process of moving away from old patterns and habits can be challenging for 7s, but they will soon find success on their path as they discover a new meaning behind a life that becomes central to all that they do. That is thanks to Neptune, which provides a source of inspiration that helps number 7s to question themselves about things such as religion or philosophy, break out of the box of the status quo, and find purpose in their new ways of looking at and doing things.

Number 8 Personality Traits

The 8 personalities are ambitious and goal-oriented. They live their lives with a sense of urgency and can be a bit impatient. 8 personalities are usually not satisfied with "just okay" but want to be the best at whatever it is that they do. They work hard to achieve success in all of their endeavors and will not settle for anything less than being the best at everything.

8's may come off as a bit abrasive or self-centered when trying to meet goals, especially if they feel like their ideas are not respected or if their goals are being challenged in some way. They need to learn how to find a balance between what they want and what is best for others instead of focusing solely on themselves all the time.

They are natural leaders and are never followers. They do not like to be controlled or manipulated by others in any way, shape, or form and will stand up for what they believe in. 8 personalities have strong convictions when it comes to making decisions and can sometimes seem unreasonable or uncompromising because of their strong sense of determination. They love to learn new things and are very interested in discovering the truth about everything. They have an extremely curious nature and love finding out how things work. Due to this, 8's make excellent inventors, researchers, scientists, etc.

They can be extremely demanding and want things done quickly and right. They want to get things done no matter what it takes or what obstacles show up along the way. They do not like to wait for results and are not afraid of taking risks to get what they want.

8's are not very good at delegating tasks but would rather do everything themselves. If a task is too big, they will break it down into smaller pieces to be easier to manage. Perhaps they should consider delegating tasks in some situations instead of trying to handle everything on their own all the time. This would free up more time for them and others to enjoy doing other things as well.

8's tend to procrastinate, especially when it comes to doing something that does not appeal to them. If a task is unpleasant or boring for an 8 personality, then it will be put off until the last minute. 8 personalities need to learn how to manage their time properly not to have stressful moments like this in the future. 8's are more sensitive and sentimental than most people. They are in tune with the feelings of others and can be easily hurt if someone is insensitive to them or if someone does something inconsiderate. They need to learn how to communicate their feelings more assertively so that others can understand where they are coming from without things getting too heated or emotional.

8 personalities are charismatic leaders who possess charisma, strength, courage, and ambition – all the qualities of a true leader. They are not afraid of being criticized by others or taking charge when necessary; they will do what needs to be done for everyone to come out as a winner.

Saturn's Influence on Number 8

In the Chaldean Numerology system, Saturn is said to create strong, steadfast, and brave people. Because of Saturn, 8's have a deep sense of justice and righteousness. They believe they have a divine right to dole out justice because they are already protecting it by being such morally-correct beings.

Chaldean Numerology Table

Curious about what the numerical value of each letter is in Chaldean numerology? Here you go:

1 2 3 4 5 6 7 8

A B G D E U O F

Q R C M H V Z P

Y K L T N W

I S X

J

You've probably noticed the absence of the number 9, and we've already gone over why. It's not that it has no symbolism; occultists recognize this number as the highest sphere, the very representation of divinity itself; therefore, it requires no letter to represent it. Having said that, when it does happen that someone's name adds up to a 9, or the compound numbers 27, 18, 36, and so on, you can ascribe the traits of 9 to them.

Chapter 3: Understanding Compound Numbers

In all numerology systems, numbers tend to have the same traits and meanings, but the thing about Chaldean numerology is that you need a lot more than just what each number means on its own. That is, you have *compound numbers.*

The numbers we went over in the previous chapters are just single or root numbers, also called *principal numbers.* However, it's time to talk about the compound or double numbers. These numbers can give you so much insight into your life. It's the meat of the topic of Chaldean numerology, but don't let that fact scare you away because you can understand them with just a bit of study and time.

While the single numbers will show you how others perceive you in your life, the compound numbers will reveal the hidden drives and motives that lead you to act the way you do. Studying them closely can give you some clues about your future or what you're fated to accomplish in life.

Every number from 10 onwards makes up double numbers. Let's say you're looking at compound number 13, for instance. You could break that down to a root of 4 by adding both digits, but having said that, 1 and 3 make up a compound number with its own unique meaning different from the root number.

The Compound Numbers

Number 10: This is represented by the Wheel of Fortune, and as a compound number, it represents the ideas of trust, confidence in yourself, and being honorable in all that you do. It's also about how you can rise as easily as you can fall. Number 10 is a number that is recognized for its potential for good or evil. How you express it in your life depends on your desires and how you choose to bring them to life. In Chaldean numerology, this is considered a number that can bring you great fortune, meaning whatever it is you seek to accomplish in life is likely to play out according to plan.

Number 11: This number has quite a bit of danger attached to it, so much so that some people recommend changing your name if you get this compound number in it. People who have this as a compound number have to live a life fraught with betrayal and treachery. It is represented by the Muzzled Lion or the Clenched Hand. If this is you, you might find that your life is full of many challenges.

Number 12: This number represents the archetype of the Victim or Sacrifice. It's a number that is ruled by anxiety and restlessness, and it often implies that one may need to go through all sorts of sacrifices on account of others, whether that's to help them or just because your struggles would entertain them.

Number 13: This number represents the energy of Death riding on a horse with its scythe, which it uses to harvest souls for the other side, and is depicted with the symbol of the Skeleton. The essence of this number is *change.* This wave of change could come in many ways, from you having to change your plans, where you live, and so on. However, don't let this change scare you because *change is not always bad.* When you accept this, you'll have mastery over everything that comes your way. Sure, change can bring destruction and totally alter the world as you've always known it, but with that destruction comes the chance to begin anew and be better than ever. This number also represents power, which is in itself neutral but can create good or bad results, depending on how you wield it. This number warns you to expect the unexpected and to make peace with the unknown when it shows up as one of your compound numbers.

Number 14: This number represents the idea of movement. It's about how things, people, and ideas can be combined to create something new. It's also about the danger that Mother Nature can present, such as fires, tornadoes, floods, etc. Don't let this number scare you, though, because it's absolutely great when it comes to matters involving your finances, business changes, and making calculated guesses in money matters. However, if this is your number, it doesn't mean you should get too cocky because there's always an element of risk involved, not because of you but because of those around you who could do some foolish things that might jeopardize your outcomes. So, you should take the necessary precautions.

Number 15: This number represents mystery and magic. It's a very important one to occultists, but not because it's the grandest. It's that whoever has this number has access to the power of magic, and they're a natural at wielding it to accomplish whatever they set out to do. When this number is connected to a principal with good ideas, this could be extremely fortunate for you. However, when it's connected to numbers like 4 or 8, it means you might not have any issues walking on the darker side of magic. Usually, those under the influence of this compound number have the gift of the gab. They're great at all forms of art and music, and when they're in the mood, they can give some drama as they have quite an interesting temperament and have an uncanny way of pulling people close to them without trying. They never have to worry about money, and for some reason, people are more than happy to do them favors even without them asking.

Number 16: This number is connected to the Tower tarot card, and you could call it the "shattered citadel." Number 16 says that you need to be careful of dangerous things to come, especially regarding the plans you've outlined for your life. It's about your future and serves as a warning that you need to be very mindful to plan for contingencies well in advance so that you don't wind up in troublesome situations that could have been avoided.

Number 17: This number is represented by Venus and her 8-pointed star, which is the epitome of Peace and Love. Some call her the Star of the Magi, which should tell you just how spiritual the number 17 is. When you're born under the influence of this compound number, it means that you've overcome all challenges in your spiritual life and your professional life as well. You have arrived at true immortality in every sense of the word, and your name will live on long after you're gone. As long as there's no connection to numbers 4, 8, and other compound numbers that can be broken down to those two numbers, this number is a very good one that will bring those under its influence luck and good fortune in all they do.

Number 18: This number has a very interesting symbolism connected to it: a moon and its rays dripping with blood, while beneath it are a dog and a wolf. Both animals are starving, ravenous with their mouths open to catch the blood that falls. Then there's a crab that wants to be a part of the action. What does this bizarre symbol mean, and how is it connected to the number 18? Well, it represents the idea that when one isn't careful, the material can completely obliterate all spiritual progress. This number is connected to issues like war and fights, from internal and personal to interpersonal and between entire nations. It seeks to warn you to expect deception and betrayal at every turn, and it could also represent the perils of Mother Nature herself. When this number shows up when you're figuring out the favorability of the date, it means you need to be careful and exercise a lot of caution on that day.

Number 19: This is a very fortunate number that, when reduced to a single number, gives you 1, which represents the sun. Represented as the Prince of Heaven, when this number shows up for you, it means you can expect success in all you do. It means that you'll be very happy indeed and that your blessings will be so obvious that others can't help but notice them and be affected by them, for better or worse. It's a good idea to make plans for your future because there's a chance that things will work out wonderfully for you.

Number 20: 20 is the Judgment or the Awakening number, if you prefer. It has to do with finding new things, whether that's a new sense of purpose, new accomplishments, new plans, and a renewed love for life. It's a number that calls for you to reach for the stars because your purpose is far grander than anything you could imagine. This number isn't about material success. In fact, it's doubtful that that's where you'll excel. When you work with this number to plan your future, you'll learn that it's warning you about possible snags in your plans, and you should be on the lookout for them. The way to overcome any hiccups is by working with your spiritual side because it is in spirit that you'll triumph.

Number 21: This number is represented by the Crown of the Magi or the Universe. It represents the idea that no matter what you do, you're always moving forward. It's about constant elevation and receiving the honor for what you accomplish, and if this number is yours, it signifies the fact that no matter how hard and long you've been struggling, success will inevitably be yours. This success is something that you can only attain after you've repeatedly demonstrated that you're never going to give up no matter what life throws your way. It's a number that calls you to remain hopeful and stay loyal to your cause.

Number 22: This number warns you that you're susceptible to being taken for a fool because of the goodness of your heart. It's a number that implies you might assume you're some sort of Pollyanna in a world where nothing goes wrong, and you'll only become aware of your delusion when you find yourself surrounded by mountains of danger. Usually, these delusions can be fueled by those who offer their incorrect opinions and judgment.

Number 23: This number promises you success in everything, especially because you're likely to receive assistance from those who are more influential or powerful than you. Making plans with this number in mind implies a lot of success.

It is known as the Royal Star of the Lion.

Number 24: This number is a good one too. It tells you that those who have the means necessary for you to accomplish what you want will come through for you, and it means you're likely to find this success by way of love, particularly with the opposite sex.

Number 25: this number represents the idea of strength through all situations and the good things that can come your way when you choose to speak less and watch more, observing what people say and do and how things play out. Now, this isn't a particularly fortunate number in the sense that all of the successful outcomes that come your way are likely to result from much struggle and tribulation in the earlier part of your life.

Number 26: This is a number that is rife with warnings about one's future, telling you to be prepared for possible issues, ruin, and disasters. This trouble is often brought about by the partnerships you get into, other people's opinions, and the terrible advice they may offer you.

Number 27: This number is about the idea of being in charge. It's about having power and wielding it in a position of authority. It also indicates that you'll get good results due to your sharp mind and the creativity that flows from you. You'll do far better executing your own plans than doing what someone else suggests when you have this compound number. You should follow the path that is true to you.

Number 28: This is an interesting number with so many conflicting ideas. For instance, it holds great potential for greatness, yet it also suggests that potential can easily be snuffed out unless you plan for your future. It also seems to indicate that the way you may be overcome by loss is by trusting other people, having to compete, and dealing with enemies all around you. Other issues could come from the law not being on your side, and there's always the chance that you'll constantly have to start over and over.

Number 29: *This is not a good number at all.* It indicates a path filled with sudden unforeseen danger, struggles, friends that simply can't be trusted, much to cry and lose sleep over, being deceived by those of the opposite sex, and more.

Number 30: This number inspires you to be retrospective and use what you glean from your past to consider what may come in the future. It implies that your mental acumen is far above and beyond those around you, so much so that you may not consider material things at all. So, this isn't an unlucky number, and it's not fortunate either. It all comes down to the way you think of your life. It could be as powerful as you want it to be.

Number 31: This shares some of the same attributes as number 30, but the difference is that when the number influences you, you're more likely to be on your own for the most part. Keep in mind that it's not the best number to have when it comes to matters of the material aspect of life.

Number 32: This is magical, similar to the number 5, or all compound numbers that add up to 5. If you're the sort of person who can maintain your own original thoughts and reservations about things, this is a great number. However, if other people's ideas and opinions easily sway you, you're very likely to suffer due to their foolishness.

Number 33: On its own, there's no power in this number. However, it is very similar in meaning to the number 24, and it's also connected to the number 6.

Number 34: This number carries the same frequency as number 25.

Number 35: This number means the same thing as 26.

Number 36: This one's the same as 27.

Number 37: This number has its own power. A number says you'll have great fortune when it comes to love and friendship, and you'll have great luck with those of the opposite sex as well. When this number shows up in terms of partnerships, it's a very good thing indeed.

Number 38: This has the same meaning as 29.

Number 39: This is the same as number 30. They both reduce to the single digit 3.

Number 40: This carries the same meaning as 31.

Number 41: This means the same thing as 32.

Number 42: It's the same thing as 24.

Number 43: This number carries a lot of bad luck, and its energy is all about failure and struggle. It also represents the idea of change, which leads to a complete overhaul of everything you've ever known. It's not a great number to make plans around.

Number 44: This means the same thing as 26.

Number 45: This is the same as 27.

Number 46: This is the same as 37.

Number 47: this is the same as 29.

Number 48: this is the same as 30.

Number 49: This carries the same frequency as number 31.

Number 50: This means the same as 32.

Number 51: This is a powerful number that carries the energy of being a warrior. It tells you that you're likely to have rapid progress whatever you decide to do, which is a great thing for you, particularly if you're a leader.

Number 52: This is the same as 43.

The previous represents all 52 weeks. Now, let's work with the symbolism of these double numbers and the single numbers.

Chapter 4: Your Destiny Numbers

The destiny number is very important in Chaldean numerology, and it's also known as your Name Number because it comes from your name. It's what helps people figure out your character, what you desire most out of life, what holds you back, and what you must do to make your dreams come true. In other words, if you want to know why you're on this little blue dot, you need to take a close look at your destiny number. You could be finding a lot of success at whatever you're involved in right now, but that doesn't necessarily mean that's what you're here for, or you may not find much joy despite how well you're doing. All you have to do is add all the numbers that make up each letter of your name. You keep adding the results you get until you have just one digit left.

Why the Destiny Number Matters

You need to know this number because it will reveal the path to success, but it will also show you exactly what you need to do to become self-actualized in life. It also shows you how you tend to handle the circumstances that present themselves in your life, whether favorable or unfavorable. You'll learn whether you're the sort of person who likes to take the bull by the horns and address things head-on or whether you're more the kind of person who likes to go with the flow and see where things lead. The number will also show you how it is you deal with the people in your life.

Now it's not always easy to work with your destiny number because there are times when what you think you should be doing isn't what your destiny number is asking of you. It's better to trust it because it's the epitome of what your higher self truly wants, and it's the pathway to your greatness.

Your Destiny Number versus Your Birth Number

Anyone who wants to know who they really are would do well to know their numbers. For instance, let's assume you were born 11-10-1973. When you add all the numbers to your birthday, you'll get your destiny number. So, in this example, here's what you'd get:

$1 + 1 + 1 + 0 + 1 + 9 + 7 + 3 = 23$

$2 + 3 = 5$

This would imply that you have 5 as your destiny number.

While the birth number talks about the body and character, the destiny number will show what you're likely to experience, how you relate with others, and how your life will likely end. If you have a destiny number that's more influential than your birth number, that means even your physical traits and character will depend on the destiny number and not the birth number.

Your birth number may reveal what your status is in life and what it is your heart yearns for the most, but the destiny number is the one that will let you know just how far you can make it in life and what hand fate will deal you. However, this doesn't mean you should be afraid of your fate because you can still thrive even within the set parameters your destiny number offers you. The trick is to make sure you're in a field that is more suited to you than whatever it is you're doing if you're not already on your path. When you work so hard in a field that isn't yours, you'll experience many obstacles along your path. This is sometimes what happens with those who constantly are beset by failure or those who finally make it after eons of struggle only to turn around and lose it all when they finally "make it."

Destiny Number 1

This destiny number is the one that has to do with leadership in all aspects of life. If this is your destiny number, it means you're usually self-sufficient, and everything you do is driven by your own thoughts and desires and no one else's. You love nothing more than to be ahead of the curve, and you naturally are. People with this destiny number don't play games in their professional life, and they're usually the ones leading the pack. The same can be said for their personal life as well. They are excellent people managers, so they can run a business just fine and have all the skills and personality traits of a powerful, successful leader. The only trouble with this number is that there's a chance people under its influence will be heavily influenced by ego. This could show up in several ways, such as selfishness, an inability to really feel what others are going through, and being a little too hard on others who aren't as gifted as they are. So, it can make them some of the most difficult partners to deal with.

When it comes to their love life, they tend to be the more dominant partner. In other words, if their partner is also dominant, there may be many issues to contend with in that relationship. This may not be a problem for those with this destiny number because usually, they don't really care much for romance, to begin with. This is just one more reason that they are best suited to someone who is submissive and willing to allow them to do as they please, supporting them in all they do.

No one is exempt from having experiences that lead to dramatic changes that could lead us to our destiny. Those under the influence of Destiny number one will have to deal with certain circumstances that will show them how willing they are to call upon a higher power to help them be more of an individual in all they do. They may not always start off being so dominant and assertive, but there will come a time when they must make that choice in life. Just like the rest of us, they have lessons that Karma must teach them. The key lesson for people with this destiny number is that the world is about other things besides themselves. Their ultimate assignment is to figure out how they can still be in leadership and an individual while making sure they are not hurting other people in the process. This is a lifelong process that will require a lot of creativity on their part.

Destiny Number 2

Those born under the influence of this number tend to be agreeable in general. Unlike number one, they are always willing to work with other people and don't have a problem submitting. They make the most excellent followers and partners you could ever ask for. If this is your destiny number, the idea behind how you can succeed in life is to work with other people just like the moon works with the light of the sun.

People with this destiny number tend to be quite the diplomat. They always find the perfect way to get their message across without stepping on toes and while achieving what they want. They are naturally kind and empathetic people who speak with grace and are gentle in all they do. They have a very strong connection to their intuition and are uncannily sensitive to the energies around them. This strong sensitivity makes them opposed to any form of conflict and makes being agreeable the easier option for them all the time.

Because these kinds of people are always willing to work with others, making them the most loving partners you could ever have. In love, whenever confronted with a situation that proves problematic, they have the ideology that it is "you and me versus the problem" and not "you versus me." They aren't interested in winning at all costs but are more invested in creating win-win situations for everyone involved. This is just one of many reasons why for number 2's, their relationships tend to last really long. Whether it's business or their love life, they make sure the foundations of the relationships that they create are very solid.

2's can be very affectionate people. If you would love someone who nurtures you through whatever you're going through and will always show you that they care with no unnecessary mind games, this is the person you want by your side. However, you need to keep in mind that they are often drawn to those who are more dominant. This sort of balance is what makes their relationships work in the long term — As long as the dominant person does not take advantage of the number 2's submissiveness. If this destiny number influences you, it is best to be with a partner who will appreciate how supportive you are and won't take advantage of your goodness.

As a number 2 person, you are very spiritual and intuitive, and you also take quite easily to esoteric matters. Odds are you have very strong psychic abilities. Usually, you are blessed with this gift because you aren't the best at being dominant. So it is much more helpful for you to detect when people are toxic from a spiritual level so that you do not get sucked into their nonsense on account of how dominating they are. It's quite possible that you weren't always in touch with your psychic abilities in your past life, which led to you being in so much trouble. That is why this time around, you find it absolutely impossible to ignore it when the divine is speaking to you.

You would do extraordinarily well in careers that involve spirituality and counseling. Anything that involves helping people or artistically expressing yourself is also a good fit. Whichever of these you choose, the fact of the matter is that everything you do will touch people in a very profound way.

Destiny Number 3

This number is strongly connected to creativity. When you put the power of the previous two together, what you get is this destiny number's energy. In other words, light and dark together will birth unrivaled creativity. The influence of Jupiter on this number means that those who are controlled by this number can create something magnificent by working with the primordial forces of life.

Destiny 3 is connected to creativity.
https://pixabay.com/es/photos/pintura-maquillaje-ni%C3%B1a-2985569/

The interesting thing about people born under number 3 is that they tend to be really radiant in person. If you could take a peek into their minds, you would find them full of brilliant ideas. They are as joyful as they are smart, too. If this is you, you don't have any problem expressing your actual thoughts, and you are very confident about yourself in all you do. You are a very avid learner, and no matter what it is you are consuming, it is not hard for information to stick. Because of this learning ability, you are very creative and artistic. Number 3's tend to have quite a sense of humor. They make some of the very best writers and musicians. They could also go into art if they want to. There's really no limit to the different ways in which they can work with their gifts.

When it comes to matters of the heart, this number does not have a problem drawing people in. Everyone loves them and wants to be around them. They have a fine balance between dominance and submission, and they know how to dance back and forth between the two to allow for peace, love, and understanding in their relationships. If this is you, the only reason you ever get into relationships with other people is simply for the sheer joy of connecting with others. However, you are not shy about pulling the trigger and ending things quickly if you notice that you are not being honored in the relationship.

Being born under the influence of this number means that you sometimes have to deal with a fair bit of struggle. It is the eternal dilemma of the starving artist. Your job is to trust that your higher self is well aware of the plan it has set out for you and that it will work out beautifully as long as you answer its call.

Destiny Number 4

Those born under the influence of this number tend to be the most practical people, and you could never accuse them of not being hard working. Four is the number of productivity. Therefore, there is nothing that these people do better than get things done. This number also represents the idea of completion. It is a number that represents the importance of maintaining proper structure and ordering everything correctly so that the world doesn't descend into chaos or remain in it for too long.

If you were born under the influence of this number, your mind is probably more concerned with material issues. This can be an incredibly good thing for you, especially in your career. The odds are that you'll hold a significant amount of power in your business. Your energy is similar to destiny number one in this way, so you tend to be in managerial positions, or at least you would thrive if you were in charge. You're the sort of person who doesn't mind ticking off a few people now and then if it means that you'll get the job done.

Your passion for love may spill over into your personal, romantic life. If you have a partner, your concern would be what's going on at work rather than what's going on at home. When you share some sort of emotional connection with someone, it'll be at work. This might make it really hard for you to actually build something that will last a lifetime. You might notice that you're drawn to those who have destiny number 1.

Your challenge is to make sure that you are not consumed by materialism. This is especially the case if you have a soul urge number that indicates you have a much larger purpose of fulfilling here in this incarnation. You must realize that the only reason you seek out material things is that you think that in getting them, you'll be happy. However, given enough time, you'll come to find that there is more to life than just the material, and going beyond this is where your true joy lies.

Destiny Number 5

The number 5 indicates that there is disorder or chaos on the horizon. It also means that you are quite free and open. However, this same freedom can be quite destructive to your long-term plans and goals if you do not exercise more control over it.

Those born under 5 venture heavily into something to give their lives meaning. These people have a strong belief system, and they tend to be very idealistic about what they see the world as needing to be like. Their supportive nature is made up of a bright, positive outlook which makes them great ways to motivate others around them or encourage them to do things.

The life path of a number 5 is full of adventure. They tend to be the live-for-the-moment people who will do something completely new or go to the extreme simply because they are bored. As long as they are having fun doing it, they will not have any problem going out on a limb or trying something that may seem absolutely ridiculous.

The challenge for anyone born under this number is to keep your head before taking off your seatbelt. You have to make sure that you know exactly what it is that your life purpose is here and now, and you have to adhere strictly to this idea. When you resist the voices of reason, you can fall into trouble. You have to realize that when you take unnecessary risks and make hasty decisions out of boredom, you can hurt yourself or others. It's not really your fault because this is who you are and what you are meant to be. The best way to live up to your true potential is by making sure that a wise mentor guides you in your life.

Destiny Number 6

People born under destiny number 6 are all about being in control, and for a good reason. This is the most aggressive of the numbers, and this is because it represents confrontation. Your challenge with this number is to make sure that you don't provoke the very people you want to help by trying to do something in your life that they will find difficult to accept.

You are definitely going to be a leader when it comes down to it, and you can be a pretty beneficial influence on others because of it. However, you need to be careful not to get so embroiled in power because, before long, you won't know how to share with others and who needs your help.

It is always a good idea to keep in mind that you have a soul tendency number that tells you that you are meant to champion today's most important issues. If you choose to ignore this, the odds are that your life will not be as fulfilling as it could have been otherwise. For example, if you choose not to help people because they don't follow your ideals, you are only hurting yourself. Your real challenge is finding a balance between helping many people and working to change the world for the better by any means necessary.

Destiny Number 7

Destiny number 7 people are very much about family and tradition. Like 5, 7 represents the idea of destiny which means that you are likely to have a strong legacy to uphold, or at least continue. Your family is very important to you, and you value their input. If it isn't them, it's your religion or community.

Destiny number 7 people make great parents because they believe in everything children choose to do in their lives. You'll be there for them through thick and thin, no matter what, even if it means that you have to sacrifice a little bit of yourself at the end of the day. The number 7 is very different and unique because it represents that you are both a leader and also the loner of the group. This can make you feel like you're floating between two worlds.

You have both strong leadership qualities but at the same time are attracted to those who lean towards more of a *freedom aesthetic* in their lives. You are also attracted to people who have big ideas and powerful beliefs that they're passionate about. This can make you somewhat of an idealist, and as someone who wants to help others find meaning in their lives or wants to live out your own purpose, you find no equal in this world.

For you, the challenge presented by this number is to actually follow through on the very strong ideas you have. It might be hard sometimes, but if you stick to your guns and find a way to get others to go with you, it may be worthwhile in the end.

Destiny Number 8

Destiny number 8 people are all about the power of love, and in some ways, this can be a little bit of a curse for them. This is especially true if they have an adventurous side they'd like to fulfill, like 5 or 6. These people tend to be very free-spirited in their younger years, but they usually start to get more serious as they get older.

People under this number tend to take their relationships very seriously, either positive or negative. Their relationship with themselves is also important because it helps them determine how much faith they will have in their personal judgments when it comes down to making decisions throughout life. If they're lucky, they will have a great balance between this and be able to make the right choices no matter what.

The challenge presented to you as a number 8 is to make sure that you don't let your relationships with other people have such a huge impact on your life. You have a lot of power in your hands, and you mustn't make the wrong decision simply because it will affect things with others. You need to stay true to yourself and not let others steer you in any direction, even if this means taking some risks.

The number 8 represents a more spiritual approach where you focus on using your own powers and abilities. You are also focused on defending what you believe in and your personal purpose in life. This can make the world around you seem strange at times because it's not always clear what things mean or how they might work out. You probably have a strong idea of what sort of things you're searching for, but you might not be too certain about all the details in your life yet. Instead of getting distracted by others' opinions or advice, you are much better off focusing on what helps you grow.

Chapter 5: Your Heart's Desire Number

Your Heart's Desire number is also known as your soul urge number, and it's the number that lets you know what it is you desire the most out of life. To calculate it, all you have to do is add all the vowels in your name, present, or given. For instance, say your name is Jennifer Wallace. You would be adding the numerical values of the following letters: E, I, E, A, A, and E. Here's the math:

1 + 5 + 1 + 1 + 5 = 13

1 + 3 = 4

Therefore, your soul urge or Heart's Desire number is 4. Let's take a look at the meaning of each number.

Heart's Desire Number 1

One is the most personal of all numbers. It's the number of wisdom and knowledge. The number one person is often the most studious or business-oriented, and they thrive on theoretical knowledge that can be applied to solving practical problems. The Heart's Desire for this person is a thirst for knowledge and understanding. Their life goal may be to accumulate as much information as possible or take everything they know and use it creatively to achieve success.

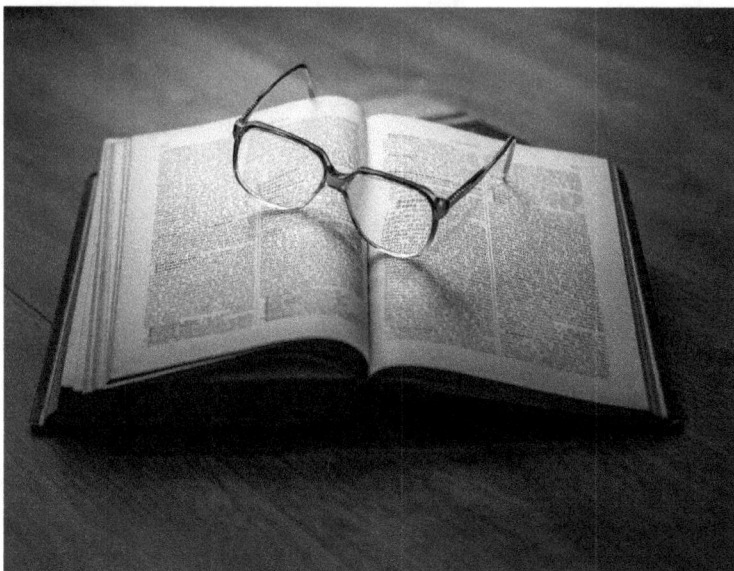

Heart's Desire 1 is known to be very intellectual.

Those born under the influence of this number are some of the most authentic people you'll ever meet, and they're also fiercely independent. You want nothing more than to take the lead or be the first to explore new grounds. When you're working with your Heart's Desire number, you're rather ambitious to the point of wanting to keep a tight leash on everything and everyone, and you can be quite the taskmaster, singularly focused on whatever you've decided is important. You desire nothing more than accomplishments and success in life.

You're an amazing achiever, and you can be a real powerhouse when you set your sights on something. It's important to note that your Heart's Desire number will tend to make others around you second guess their own dreams; use this influence gently and with care. You know what your heart desires, and it'll stop at nothing to have it. This is not always the best way to go, as it may cause others in your life great distress. If you're truly working toward what you want, then you won't harm another to achieve it. Sometimes, just because someone else doesn't understand what makes us happy doesn't mean they don't deserve our respect.

Heart's Desire Number 2

Two is the total opposite of the number one. It deals with relationships and teamwork. Two is highly adaptable and very personable. This individual is extremely sociable, always looking for a way to be with others. They love learning from those around them and want nothing more than to feel truly connected to the people around them at all times. Because their desires are based on the needs of others, they must focus on what's most important in life - each other. If your heart's desire is a successful relationship or great community connections, this number will help you reach those goals by helping you understand what makes others tick.

The number two person is often a true artist. They are highly expressive and always charming. The Heart's Desire for this person is also to be admired and adored by others. They want to know that they are loved and appreciated by those around them. They love to spread light and warmth wherever they go, and their influence is infectious. People tend to be very fond of the second person, probably because their warm smile creates a strong positive vibe that draws others naturally in.

Those under the influence of this number will have a natural ability to bring out the best in people. This generous and loving soul never hesitates to make you feel good about yourself, even if you need a little reassurance. You tend to be charitable and gracious with your time and money, valuing love and security over material possessions. You may be inclined toward helping those in need, whether they're strangers or family. You've got a big heart and are always interested in hearing what others have to say; you must learn to listen well before you speak so that you don't offend anyone unintentionally. You're a natural peacemaker and often see both sides of an argument or situation.

Heart's Desire Number 3

If you've got a Heart's Desire number of 3, you're a born salesperson and have the gift of gab. You're excellent at building connections and networking, but you might focus on that instead of your own needs. Your greatest strengths are your intelligence, charisma, artistic vision, and intuition. You'll need to be more realistic with your goals and not always focus on what others want from you. You love nothing more than teamwork, and it's important to you that you are allowed to express yourself, especially in writing. You're a born entertainer and will always be the center of attention.

You're imaginative and enjoy pursuing goals that are based solely on your imagination instead of reality. Sometimes, this can cause you to neglect your own needs. The heart's desire for this person is a life full of adventure, travel, and fun. This person is extremely creative, as they have both artistic flair and business savvy. They're likely to have a great deal of success at getting others on board with their plans because they can use their natural charisma to get their way through all sorts of situations. This generous soul won't hesitate to help someone in need.

The 3 is a natural when it comes to making conversation. They have a knack for drawing others in and making them feel comfortable enough to share their deepest thoughts. This is the perfect person to turn to in a time of crisis; they're more than happy to listen and provide support as needed. Be careful not to take advantage of their natural friendliness, as they can be quite gullible at times and may believe what they hear without questioning its validity. People born under this number should focus on handling issues head-on instead of simply ignoring the problems or brushing them aside with flattery or small talk.

Heart's Desire Number 4

The number 4 is capable of accomplishing great things. They have a lot of potential, so this number loves to try new things and learn more about their surroundings. If you're Heart's Desire number 4, you're bold and blunt with your point of view. You can be a little too direct at times but will make up for that with your sharp mind and supporting abilities. As they develop, you gravitate towards different areas of life and enjoy being methodical with how you approach each one.

Number 4s are ambitious, hardworking, and intelligent, which helps them achieve great success in their chosen career. They're very detail-oriented and organized, but they may struggle with their own self-worth and confidence at times. They're highly skilled workers who put everything into achieving their goals. This person is an idealist and a dreamer, which is both a blessing and a curse. Because they don't always look at the facts realistically, they tend to be disappointed when things don't pan out as planned. The Heart's Desire number four focuses on artistry, excellence in workmanship, and accomplishment in life.

You've got a tendency to be overly critical of yourself, so you may need to work on accepting yourself for who you are. People with this number tend to be perfectionists that strive for excellence in everything they do. They must smile more often; this is a caring soul, and the smallest things tend to bring them joy. They're very loyal and dedicated, making them valuable employees. A Heart's Desire of four indicates that this person thrives in situations where they work alongside others toward a common goal. This person aims to be pragmatic in all their ways, and they can sometimes take perfectionism to the extreme. If this is you, your ultimate desire is stability in life.

Heart's Desire Number 5

The 5 brings the gift of enthusiasm. They're caring and compassionate souls who love to help those around them. People tend to treat them with respect and admiration, as they're reliable and honest. Their enthusiasm can be contagious, encouraging others to do their best as well. You have a talent for communicating with passion and enthusiasm, making you a great public speaker or writer.

The Heart's Desire number 5 is usually very optimistic about their future, which makes them an excellent speaker or speaker coach because they know exactly what to say at each moment to capture your attention. They tend to be very creative, although sometimes their creative ideas can clash with reality — which the ego has a lot of power over at times. To the disappointment of many, they usually don't learn from their mistakes and tend to repeat them (which isn't all bad, as it often leads to another creative idea). The heart's desire of five is about being at ease with themselves and others.

You've got a lot of potential; you must spend more time considering how you can put your skills to good use. Five indicates that this person is happiest in situations where they're working alongside others toward a goal or mission. They're easily able to motivate those around them, making them successful leaders in any profession. This generous soul loves helping those around them, especially in times of need.

Heart's Desire Number 6

The 6 is a homebody and is quite content with the simple things in life. They enjoy being around others but can become too attached to the details of their surroundings. You're usually very laid-back, making it easy for you to stay calm even under pressure. These 6s tend to be shy about sharing their secrets, but they're a great listener and always welcome the opportunity to help someone else in need. You may have a deep fear of failing or letting others down; it's important that you face these fears head-on instead of avoiding them altogether.

The Heart's Desire number six is usually very caring. They have a knack for making others feel special, and they're always looking to help when they can. The number six is very grounded in reality, making them excellent organizers and planners. They tend to be knowledgeable in their chosen field of work, enabling them to truly shine. They're sincere and honest, which has led them to gain the respect of many with their natural ability to help others.

They're usually very organized and practical, which makes them great at delegating tasks to those around them. They're also honest and straightforward, making it easy for them to relate to others professionally and personally. The Heart's Desire number six wants to help others achieve their dreams, providing support in any way they can.

Heart's Desire Number 7

The number seven is a natural for the arts and the humanities. They're intelligent, thoughtful individuals who love taking risks with their work. This is a very philosophical soul who can talk for hours about the various intricacies of life. They've got a lot of creativity and ingenuity, but they may sometimes struggle with their own self-doubt and feelings of inadequacy. They tend to be far more successful when they let others take the lead at times, as they may be too distracted by their own thoughts to pay attention to what matters most.

The Heart's Desire number seven is usually very affectionate and charming. This person hates being alone; with that said, you must keep your wandering mind in check because it sometimes leads them away from the present moment instead of focusing on what really matters most in life. You're typically very optimistic about the future, which makes you an excellent leader — but only if you can keep your thoughts organized.

Life may not be perfect, but it's still pretty good for someone with your number. Seven indicates that this person is happiest in situations where they're working on a creative or philosophical project alongside others who share their interest in the arts and humanities. This is an idealistic soul who's always seeking new adventures and fresh approaches to life. They love to challenge themselves, which sets them apart from many of their peers. The Heart's Desire number seven thrives on self-expression and strives to follow their passions.

Heart's Desire Number 8

The number eight is often seen as very enthusiastic and spontaneous, but they also need time alone to recharge their batteries. They're usually very capable of making good decisions for themselves, but they don't always take the time to consider the big picture because they tend to get wrapped up in their own world. The number eight is highly intuitive and empathetic, and they make an excellent judge of character. This person admires strong leaders and strives to be the ideal leader themselves.

The Heart's Desire number eight is all about inner peace. The number eight is an excellent choice for business owners, investors, or entrepreneurs. They're great leaders and are very logical in their approach to life. They love being in charge but often underestimate the value of teamwork. The ego has a lot of power over this person, which can cause them to be defensive at times. On the flip side, they're very loyal and dedicated to those they love most, making them one of the most loving and generous souls you'll ever meet.

The Heart's Desire number eight is usually very wise and mature for their age. This very creative person understands that not all their ideas will work out the first time around. They're unique and can take people by surprise, making them a great entertainer. The number eight tends to struggle when it comes to acceptance and admiring others, so you must learn to be more confident in your abilities. The ego can also cause this person to be too sensitive at times, leading to unnecessary jealousy or anger.

How to Interpret Compound Numbers

Let's go back to our example with the name Jennifer Wallace. We got the compound number 13 and the Heart's Desire number 4. How do you combine both interpretations? Let's refer to what we said about the energy of number 13. The compound number stands for change through the destruction that allows newer and better things to come your way if you adopt a positive outlook.

Meanwhile, your soul urge number 4 says you're the sort of practical and realistic person. What does this mean for you? It means you need to find some sort of balance between being rigid and flexible. The thing is that change is inevitable, and so if you refuse to be flexible in the face of it, the winds will not only bend you but break you, and that will lead to complete chaos and destruction. So, your job is to learn how to let in the new by knowing when to stand your ground. You must learn to stick to your guns versus when to let the divine take charge and trust that the upheaval causing all your plans to fall apart will lead you to a beautiful conclusion. So, practice with other names and see how you can integrate the meanings and implications of the combinations of compound numbers and heart desire numbers for those you know and love, and see how accurate you are at interpreting their charts.

Chapter 6: Your Personality Profile Number

Your personality profile number, or simply put, personality number, is a number made up of a single digit that results from all the consonants in your birth name or assigned name. You have to consider all the consonants in your first, middle, and last names for this to be accurate. This number helps you realize exactly the sort of energy you're putting out there, and you'll come to figure out why it is that things work out wonderfully with some people while they fall apart with others. Along with the other numbers on your numerology chart, this one makes up a vital part of your spirit's foundation and how it plans to express itself in this world.

So, let's assume your full name is Jennifer Amethyst Wallace. We would only be interested in the values of the following letters: J, N, N, F, R, M, T, H, S, T, W, L, L, C. Here's the math:

$1 + 5 + 5 + 8 + 2 + 4 + 4 + 5 + 3 + 4 + 6 + 3 + 3 + 3 = 56$

$5 + 6 = 11$

$1 + 1 = 2$

Remember, if you get a double-digit, you have to reduce it to just one. Let's take a look at the various personality profile numbers and what they mean. (Note, we didn't include Y in the calculation because, in this case, it serves as a vowel and not a consonant.)

Personality Number 1

The 1 personality is ambitious but focused and strives to attain what they set for themselves with no compromise. They are also very determined to achieve their goals and success. Their pride can be easily hurt when they are upset by others. The number 1 also has a natural talent for leadership and spotting potential in others who are overlooked. They have an inherent sense of duty to succeed where necessary because it's what they were put on Earth to do. They are often very charming and have a commanding presence in any room. They are very personal people and have many friends.

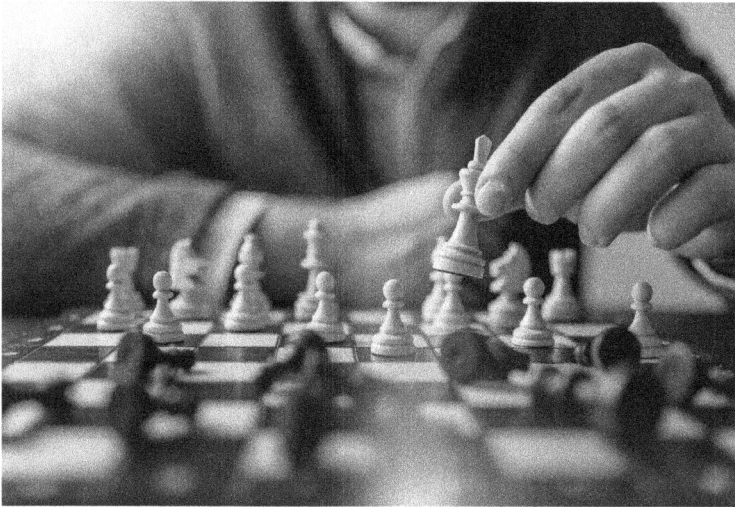

Personality 1 has the potential for leadership.
https://pixabay.com/es/photos/ajedrez-juego-estrategia-3325010/

1's like to take charge and also stand up for themselves when necessary. They love challenges and adventures, trying to see how far they can go with them. The number 1 is also very creative and likes to "fix" things around them. This can be either something small that needs fixing or a broken engine on the latest model of their car, which gets them excited because they like solving problems in a timely fashion. They like to keep people guessing, and if they can't figure out what's going on, they'll point fingers or blame someone else.

There are times, though, when they admit that they can be clueless about how something works, and it can therefore make others feel uneasy around them because everyone knows if anyone knows what to do, it ought to be them. They like to let the calls come to them rather than contacting anyone first. 1's are also very loyal people and will stick with a decision for a long time before changing their mind about an issue. They are dependable and trustworthy, so many people want to work alongside them as a partner in life. 1's always tend towards being positive people as well, always wanting the best for others in any situation that arises.

They are also not afraid of confrontation if necessary and will always tell people the truth regardless of how it might be received. The number 1 personality is also very persuasive. It has an eloquent way with words, even able to talk their way out of situations that might have otherwise ended up in a disaster. The focus on being successful plays a big role in what they do; they like to see the best outcome possible, making their workday productive rather than dull or monotonous if they have to perform repetitive tasks each day.

The number 1 is also an expert in finances and can quickly earn money. They are also extremely hard workers and put in all of the effort needed to get their work done. Sometimes 1's can be self-centered people and need to learn how to care about others more than themselves. Money is important because 1's feels it equals success. They sometimes also feel lonely or isolated from everyone around them, needing someone in their life with whom they can share their secrets.

They like to control many things in their lives, which can make it difficult when they are around others who are trying to influence them in any way. People born with this personality number also want to be admired by others and will attempt to perform as many tasks as possible that will get them the attention they need and deserve. Number 1's don't like drama or confrontation, but there are times when they can get angry quickly because of their pride. They need admiration so badly that this can cause some problems for them if they don't receive it often enough.

Personality Number 2

The 2 personality is very compassionate, loving, and kind to others. They have several good qualities, including being trustworthy and always loyal to their family. 2's are also creative, artistic, and know-how to inspire others with clever ideas for improvements on what they're doing. Perhaps the 2 personality numbers are some of the most adaptable in the world. They get along well with everyone and won't experience conflicts in any relationships, and can put aside their own needs to help improve another person's situation.

2's are very funny too, have a quick wit, and possibly tell the best jokes around. They are detectives, able to see something that other people might miss, and are a great asset when it comes to spotting anything wrong or suspicious. They provide advice based on the situation that they've seen, and everyone loves listening to what they have to say. People love their praise as well, and 2's will often be known as people who are encouraging, supportive, caring about other people's situations, and willing to provide good advice.

The trait of being a great listener also helps in this case because most 2's can keep up with whatever is being talked about with no problem at all. They are very determined people and make excellent leaders because of their natural ability in terms of compassion for others. 2's can also be very diplomatic, always wanting the best outcome possible with their words and actions. They are very determined to succeed because they have the passion and drive to succeed.

2's often put their needs second to help someone else out, which can be a great problem when people see them as selfless because of this. They sometimes may not want people around them for long periods of time because of their desire to remain alone every now and then. They will often keep secrets from others because they feel that no one really needs to know how much they really care about other people around them.

2's like to help others and do so with enthusiasm, but sometimes their sense of compassion for others can make them become awkward when dealing with other people's needs. It takes a lot of work from this personality number to be able to make others feel good about themselves and the way they're doing things. This can be a good thing because 2's are extremely loyal people and stick with their friends through thick and thin to ensure that they are always as successful as possible.

People born with this number are very creative in terms of finding new ways to do things or improve on what is already being done around them. They like to help others with their problems, but not unless they are asked to do so. 2 personalities, when not involved in any partnership, must consider others, love being in control of everything in their lives, and be very bossy at times. This can make them seem very self-centered, but it's really just a part of who they are and what makes them special.

Personality Number 3

3 personality numbers are born entrepreneurs, always wanting to improve on what is already there. They can create something new out of something that has existed for a long time (think of the internet or the wheel). They will always want to change their lives, do things differently, and find ways to do so. They can be creative and have original ideas, often seeing the possibilities in everything from the simplest of objects to a common conversation.

3's are very confident in whatever is being done or created around them. People often describe 3's as bold or assertive people because they are very good at getting what they want out of life with no problem at all. They can make fast decisions when necessary and don't always think about what other people might need before deciding. This may get them into trouble sometimes because 3's may act without thinking through all of the consequences that could come from their actions.

They can persuade others and are often known as people who enjoy being around others like them. They make good leaders, but only in groups where they can be the center of attention because they need the approval of others to feel good about themselves. The approval and admiration of other people are extremely important to the 3 personality numbers, which can sometimes make them seem as if they only care about themselves.

But really, this isn't true at all because 3's really do care a lot about others and want to be there for them whenever possible, but they just want to be admired by everyone around them so they can feel good about themselves too. They are very creative people and enjoy being able to express themselves in any way possible.

They also love being around others who they can learn while helping others with their projects. The more admiration they get from other people, the better, and this is where personality number 3 really shines. They are full of energy and love to be around others who seem as if they can go on forever without stopping until they get what they want. 3's like helping other people because it makes them feel good about themselves. They usually know how to create a positive environment that inspires greatness in those around them.

3's are people who usually want to know exactly how things are done. Introspective, they want to know their own strengths and weaknesses to succeed in whatever they do next. They will never tell anyone that something is impossible for them or that they can't make something work because they see the possibilities within everything around them. People also tend to say that 3 personalities are very outgoing, but in reality, they are very private people

Personality Number 4

4's are extremely competitive and ambitious, always wanting to be the best they can be. They love being strong and having power over others, so they can sometimes seem very domineering or even harsh. Their power comes from making others want to follow them and do what they say because of their personality number 4.

4 personalities usually have a very strong desire for power in whatever it is that they do in life. They realize that the best way for them to be successful is for everyone else to want what's best for them too, which can sometimes make people not like the 4 personality numbers because they seem so self-absorbed.

They have a strong desire to be in control but are only this way because they feel as if they need to control everything they can possibly control at all times. If a situation doesn't go the way they expect, then a 4 personality usually becomes highly upset and can become very destructive. They like to make sure that things are right and have been planned out ahead of time and will often lose their temper if things don't go exactly like they want them to.

4 personalities also tend to be very focused on material success, which is not always because they want the luxury things in life but because of their need for power over others around them. They also have a very hard time sharing control and will often have trouble letting go of the fact that they are in control of a situation. They like to help others with their problems, but only if it doesn't mean that they have to give up the control of whatever it is that they are currently in charge of.

People with this personality number can be seen as being unfeeling or uncaring because they tend to make decisions very quickly and usually don't ask for input from others when making these decisions. This can sometimes hurt people around them because 4 personalities love passionate people about what they do, but if someone else has an opposing view, then a 4 won't take long before shutting them down.

4's tend to have strong ideas and often have difficulty with change, especially if it means sacrificing their power or the things for which they have worked. They will work very hard for what they believe in, making them seem ruthless to some people when paired with their incredibly ambitious nature. But really, 4's are just as much down to earth as anyone else; they are just too focused on themselves to see this.

Personality Number 5

5's love being part of a team; because of this, they like helping others. They are very resourceful and have a bit of a problem with being able to sit still, which can sometimes lead them to procrastinate on projects. They can see things from all aspects of life, making them seem as if they are never focused on one thing long enough.

When 5's try their hardest to focus on one thing at a time is when they are most successful and can be seen as the strongest in whatever it is that they choose to do in life. They love finding new ways of doing things and don't really mind if something takes a little longer than originally planned because they enjoy seeing things grow over time instead of just rushing through everything without stopping for anything.

5's love to help others and give advice to those around them. They always tend to see things from a different point of view, and because of this, they have a hard time focusing on one thing alone for a long period of time. They love helping others who seem as if they could use the help and most likely will not say that something is impossible for them to accomplish. A 5 person will also never say that someone is wrong or just plain wrong because they believe in the fact that everyone is different, with their own strengths and weaknesses surrounding them.

A 5 personality doesn't like it when someone else tries to control what they are doing or doesn't listen to their ideas on how something should be done. They love to be given the freedom to develop their own solutions and ideas and don't like being told that they can't possibly accomplish something because they will always prove people wrong.

The 5 personality number doesn't like being wrong or acknowledging that they were incorrect on something. A person with this personality number needs to learn how to become more flexible because 5 personalities sometimes have a problem with this, especially if it means stepping out of their comfort zone. They do not like witnessing rules or laws broken, which sometimes makes them seem very uptight or strict.

5's are always looking for new things to learn and places to go, which makes the fact that they are really great at seeing things from many different angles. The 5 personality number is also very private, even though they need people they can trust around them. They can often be counted on for their advice in almost any situation.

Personality Number 6

6 personality numbers are people who love to have fun, sometimes more than anything else in the world. They have lots of friends and are very devoted to the causes that they believe in. They love to help others whenever they can but often feel as if they are not appreciated for their hard work.

6's need an array of friends and like having a million different things going on around them at all times. They love seeing how far their limits can be pushed and will go to great lengths to ensure that other people are happy before even thinking about themselves. 6's are very determined and like to do things they feel can accomplish the best. They have incredibly strong wills and will never stop in the middle of a project, even though sometimes it might be necessary to do so.

6 personalities love adventure, but not when it is at their own expense. They are rarely willing to stand up for themselves but rather tend to stick up for other people who are always wrong or who deserve what they get because of their behavior. A 6 personality is often not happy unless they are busy doing something. They love to be around others who like doing the same things that they do and will happily give up their time to make sure that everyone else is having a good time.

6's are very sensitive and have trouble dealing with confrontation; they tend to avoid arguments at all costs. They have great senses of humor and love telling jokes that make people laugh. 6 personalities do not like conflict, but it can often be seen as too passive if they don't stand up for themselves more in life. They are responsible people who always finish what they start and sometimes tend to over commit their resources to other people who cannot stand on their own feet. 6's have a hard time saying no to people who are asking for their help and tend to let their emotions get the best of them at times. They will often take opportunities that they don't need and sometimes don't even consider things like this because they can't see past the moment that they are in.

Personality Number 7

7 personalities tend to think things through and sometimes consider more than others. They are very spiritual people and love finding ways to improve themselves. They love finding the answers to any question that someone might have, which is why they excel at research.

People with the personality number 7 tend to be more romantic than most other people because they see life as something beautiful, with so many opportunities out there for everyone. They try to stay away from anything they see as negative in their lives, even though this can sometimes lead them into trouble because it can cause them to ignore a problem until it is too late or until it has become bigger than what it needed be.

7 people do not like taking risks but are more than willing to give new opportunities a try when it feels safe enough. They are very social, passionate people who love to help others as much as possible. They always try to be open about their own problems, and even though they do not want others to complain about them, they will often share their problems with those they love because they know that someone will always be there for them.

A 7 personality is usually very wise with their choices in life and always sees things in a way that is different from everyone else around them. They tend to think about their decisions before acting on them and always consider how the consequences will affect them in the end. They are not very spontaneous people and would much rather plan everything out beforehand to know what their options are at all times.

7's are very good at giving advice on almost any situation but have a hard time taking it themselves sometimes because they tend to be stubborn. They care about everyone they come in contact with, even if it is just a little bit, which makes them extremely loyal, individuals. They love to help others whenever they can without expecting anything in return and will most likely always be there for someone no matter what happens in their lives. They are also very passionate in their personal lives and tend to have difficulty separating their emotions.

Personality Number 8

8's are very quiet, shy people that do not like to be the center of attention. They love to, more often than not, just sit back and enjoy the company of others, which is why they are so good at having long-term relationships.

They tend to keep their problems to themselves instead of confiding in others about them so that they don't have anyone else around when they need someone most. They are very protective of those around them and keep watch over everyone at all times. 8's are also extremely loyal people who will stick by the person they care about no matter what happens in life. They are very grounded individuals who tend to be self-sufficient.

8's do not like being dependent on others and will go to great lengths to avoid being this way, although sometimes it might be inevitable for them. They are very optimistic people who have a good sense of humor and can often be seen laughing when nothing else is happening around them. They are very hard workers and never stop until their goal has been achieved, even if it means that they need to put in more effort than everyone else. 8 personalities love to be with someone who shares the same beliefs as they do and works at whatever they do together as much as they can.

8 personalities are very good with money and are the best when it comes to saving their funds. They tend to be more cautious than most other people because they often overanalyze every tiny detail of a situation before acting on it. It is almost impossible for them to make rash decisions, so they tend to overthink everything in their lives.

People with this personality number always try to be honest about everything around them and will not easily give someone their trust unless they really believe that this person can be trusted. They are very motivated individuals and can often be seen as stubborn because they tend to be very independent when they are around something they truly want. They have a hard time trusting people, and it is often hard for them to let go of their past decisions.

Chapter 7: Your Birthdate Number

Your birthdate number is also known as your birth number, and it is simply calculated by adding up all the digits that make it up. So, if you were born on September 2, your birth number would be 2. However, if you were born on September 14, your birth number would be 5, which is the sum of 1 and 4. Your birth number matters because it is the number that shows you everything unique about you unique. Without further ado, let's get into each one.

Birth Number 1

An individual born with a birth number of 1 is naturally confident, but it can be assumed that they are not particularly adept at facing challenges. This may be due to their innate belief that all challenges can easily be solved with their intelligence. Someone with this birth number may have had difficulties accepting and learning from past mistakes, which could hinder them in future endeavors, but never for too long because they will not quit until they've overcome the obstacles in their way. However, the risk of significantly bad outcomes is minimal given the individual's optimistic nature. In addition to that, these individuals tend to work hard towards achieving their goals because they don't give up easily; there is no challenge too large for them to overcome.

1 is a leader and initiator. This 1 can inspire those around them and get people marching in unison for a common cause. Their goal is to make sure each part of the team makes sound contributions that help the overall achievement of their value proposition. 1s are typically positive and

optimistic but also stubborn when it comes to sticking with their initial idea, even if it doesn't meet with approval from others or appears inefficient at first glance.

The number 1 stands for the self, which tells of your own ambitions and desires. Number 1, people are very discerning beings and know what is necessary for their success. They also tend to be stubborn and make decisions based on their personal needs rather than what others may want. They are not people-oriented, preferring to focus on their individual needs first before giving attention to those around them. Personal success is paramount to them, so they will have wide-ranging interests that may include business, art, or sciences.

Birth Number 2

Birth Number 2 individuals have a strong desire to be liked and accepted. However, because they tend to overindulge, they may not always make the best choices to be well-liked. They want to keep their friends and family happy by going overboard with their efforts and putting themselves in unnecessarily dangerous situations. This can lead to dramatic results when they cannot stop themselves from taking on more than they can handle. They often enjoy creative activities such as writing or music, as these allow them to express themselves freely without being judged by others.

Birth number 2 likes to be accepted.
https://pixabay.com/es/photos/gente-mujeres-hablando-re%C3%ADr-2567915/

They usually have a strong social bond and enjoy being around friends, but they know when to stop spending time with them to take care of themselves. They are very loyal people and will stick by their friends until the end. They are outspoken individuals and can be quite persuasive as well. Suppose a person with this number hasn't learned to evolve and balance out their energies. In that case, they can often become manipulative and controlling, but this only does more harm than good to their relationships.

What is birth number 2 like in love? They are very close to their partners and will give all of themselves to them. Still, they may also overindulge and become too controlling. This is a common hindrance in forming healthy relationships. 2 people who don't know any better tend to put others before themselves and will blame their partners' mistakes if it means keeping a trusted relationship intact. They believe that opening up emotionally is necessary to be happy and share their emotions with their significant other. Still, when they sense they aren't being appreciated, they clam up and can cut people off. This is usually very confusing for others who have come to take the love and support of this number for granted.

Birth Number 3

An individual with a birth number of 3 is an inspiring and energetic person who can conjure up passionate emotions from others. If a 3 doesn't motivate and inspire those around them, they will find it hard to get anything done. The fact that this number represents the mind reveals that the individual is keen on their thoughts and always has an opinion to share, even if it's not always highly supported by evidence. These people do their best work in groups, as they thrive when other people are present to listen to what they have to say and respond accordingly. They look forward to sharing creative ideas with others because having positive input helps them develop even better solutions.

These individuals are not only great conversationalists but also have a knack for writing and performing, which they usually do as a way to express themselves. 3 people often work in theater or artistic fields, but they fail to consider how others perceive their work and can thus seem insensitive. The number 3 is hot-tempered and stubborn, so they will fly off the handle if pushed too far.

3 stands for the self-expression of emotions, which tells us that these individuals may be sensitive but prone to overreact at times. They tend to be quite attached to those around them, but this attachment can make them dependent on others and decrease their ability to maintain an independent lifestyle. Three is the number of imagination and originality. The potential of the three is unlimited, and they are capable of attaining

success in any venture they choose. They are hard workers, and their can-do attitude brings them success both professionally and personally. It would seem that the glass is always half full when you are a three because they will always find something positive to say even in a situation that looks completely negative on the surface. Their natural optimism is what makes them go so far. However, like all other numbers, some inconsistencies in their lives can slow down their progress or stop them altogether.

They also symbolize the expression of energy, which is something that 3 people need to learn to do more often to release any stress from work. If a 3 person doesn't practice meditation or release their emotions, they can become quite unbalanced and may even start to develop intense headaches or a constant feeling of exhaustion. Sometimes this can result from stress in general, but if the individual never practices self-care, it could lead to something much worse.

3 people are always seeking new experiences and tend to be very philosophical about life. They can sometimes take on more than they can handle to be productive, but as long as they don't make that a habit, it isn't as big of a problem. 3 are very passionate individuals and will put all of their energy into whatever they do, whether it's work or relationships. They enjoy pleasing their partners and are anxious to form connections with others.

Birth Number 4

4 is the number of physical security and represents the material world. It may appear that a number 4 has it all together, but often this is not the case. There is always something new around the corner for a 4 person, making them feel like there isn't any real stability in their lives. They are very emotional in both the good and bad sense of the word. 4 is a number that people with a strong will often have, so they don't tend to be pushovers. They are hardwired for progression and finding ways to easily adapt to whatever comes their way to develop their skills quickly.

4 people naturally have talents in addition to their intellect. Still, sometimes they do not realize these talents in time because they lack self-confidence and focus. 4 is quite impatient and impulsive and usually takes on projects that others avoid for fear of failing, which can lead them down some dark paths that will take them away from the right path if they fail. They are mostly goal-oriented and can stay focused on what they are trying to accomplish, but they have to learn how to find a balance between their

other interests and their work.

4 is the number of work, which means that 4 people tend to be competitive in nature. They always want to be moving forward or taking the next steps up and will get anxious if they cannot accomplish anything. Because a number 4 is trying to balance their desires with the material world, they often form relationships to feel secure, which can take its toll over time.

Birth Number 5

5 represents the mind and the internal, so we tend to think of 5 people as very clever and intellectual. The number 5 is a balanced number that everyone can relate to, and it's no surprise that this number has gained so many fans throughout history. 5 has a double meaning because the first half of it symbolizes physical security while the second half refers to mental security. 5 people have an abundance of ideas and mental acuity, but this can be their downfall when they begin to confuse originality with having the right to be disrespectful of others.

They are very loyal to relationships and will always try to please others. 5 people are usually very empathetic but may be reluctant to open up emotionally because they don't want to reveal their feelings for fear of being judged. This is a sign that they hope for love from others but fear vulnerability, so they hold back on letting people close to avoid getting hurt. 5 people need to find others who understand their lack of trust to help them open up, rather than force them to defend themselves.

5 is the number of chances and represents the unexpected, so we often find 5 people being very spontaneous. They have a lot of energy but don't know how to use it effectively, so they can be quite scattered at times. People with this number also have a big imagination and usually enjoy expanding their horizons by discovering different points of view on issues that affect society as a whole. On the other hand, 5 people are often afraid of failure and can feel deeply insecure if they feel like they've let others down somehow.

Blessed with the energy of 5, many people with this number become writers and philosophers because they can think fast enough to put complex ideas into words that many others could never understand. When they decide to pursue a career, it's evident that they are intelligent enough to impact society somehow. It would be beneficial for 5 people to find ways to relax more often because their minds tend to wander when left alone for too long, which may lead them astray from the truth.

Birth Number 6

6 is the number of education and represents what we learn globally. People with 6 as their birth number are very compassionate, but they also tend to be moody because they often feel misunderstood. The fact that they are gracious to others may lead people to take advantage of them or try to use them as a doormat when things aren't going well for themselves, but if this happens enough times, 6 people can become very cynical and develop trust issues.

6 people need to remember that there is nothing wrong with being trusting, especially when it comes to other human beings. They can be a bit shy about expressing their feelings at times, but they are passionate and honest when they do. They tend to be very loving towards others and focus their energy on the people in their lives, making them feel very needed. 6 is the number of endurance, and this means that 6 people have incredible willpower and will continue to fight for what they believe in no matter what opposition comes their way.

6 people have a lot of good traits but also have a few bad ones. On the one hand, they are very intelligent and understand that everything has an endpoint, so they try to take control of situations or avoid problems altogether by thinking before acting or listening before speaking. On the other hand, 6 people can be a bit controlling and overbearing because they fear losing important things. They also like to micromanage others, but this can make them seem stubborn if they refuse to listen to others' opinions.

6 is the number of services, so 6 people are very willing to give back to their communities. They are usually very generous with their time and money, which makes them great friends and family members. 6 people spend a lot of time thinking about everything they're doing or preparing for something that's coming up soon. They are also very accepting of everything that happens and believe that there is always a positive way to look at things. Some people get tired of waiting around for 6 people to take action, which can lead them to places they don't want to go.

Birth Number 7

7 represents the past and future, so most people with the number 7 as their birth number have many ideas about what could happen in the

future and often dream about it. They tend to be extremely creative and intellectual, and many have talents that allow them to get inside other people's heads to see things from their point of view. This can make them quite empathetic, which can be good or bad depending on how they use that power.

The number 7 is the seeker of knowledge, and many people with this number will spend their entire lives trying to find out who they are inside and what makes them tick. There are times when 7 people may begin to question themselves because they don't always understand why they react to certain things in a certain way. This small amount of insecurity can cause them to overthink everything around them and question why other people behave the way they do.

7 is the number of insights, so 7 people better understand things before they happen. They are seekers of knowledge, and they understand that we live in a very complicated world where there are no easy answers. They believe that the only way to move forward is if we allow ourselves to have faith and rely on one another so we can find the answers together. This isn't a setback but rather a way for positive things to happen.

On the downside, 7 people can be quite indecisive at times because they often have so many ideas running through their minds at once that it's hard for them to focus on just one thing. They may also feel like their world has gone crazy because everything is moving too fast for them to keep up. If they can find a way to relax and take the time to enjoy life more, they will be far happier than if they spend their days overthinking.

Birth Number 8

8 is the number of prosperity, so some people with this number will have a lot of money come their way at some point in their lives. People with 8 as their birth number often do well at things like business or politics because they understand what's happening around them. They have a deep understanding that comes from experiencing life and have learned that nothing is ever truly certain unless you make it so. People with 8 as their birth number also have a deep-rooted sense of faith that helps them stay grounded when everything seems to be falling around them.

Some people with 8 as their birth number can be overly ambitious because they desperately want to make the most out of life. This is actually a good thing when they choose to use it positively and help others, but sometimes it can go to the extreme and make them seem like they care more about themselves than others. 8 is the number of ambition, so if someone with this number has too much, there may be times when they put their own needs before others.

People with 8 as their birth number are willing to take risks, and they understand that someday they will have to lose to win. They don't mind hard work because they know it's a part of life, and they enjoy having goals and a strong work ethic. They have very high moral standards, which makes them passionate about the causes they support. If someone with this number tells you that something is important, they believe it completely even if others do not.

On the downside, people with 8 as their birth number can get carried away with their ideas and make decisions based on fear rather than logic or facts. Their quick decision-making skills and the fact that they don't really care what people think or say can often lead to them making bad decisions that they regret later. If they can learn to slow down and take the time to evaluate everything, they will be much happier.

Chapter 8: Building a Numerology Chart

There's really no better way to learn about who you really are and why you're here than by working with your numerology chart. In this chapter, you'll get all the information you need to understand how these charts work and how you can create your own so that you have a clear map of your life to refer to whenever you feel afraid or lost or could use some reassurance. It's not an overly complicated process at all.

What's a Chart, Anyway?

Where Chaldean numerology is all about understanding the underlying meaning of each number, both principal and compound, the chart is basically a summary of everything to do with every number connected to who you really are. Judging from all the information you've received in the previous chapters, you can tell that the level of detail in these charts is not to be trifled with. But it's really an easy thing to put the meanings of these numbers side by side and then come up with an explanation for what's happening with you, as we did in a previous chapter.

Requirements for Your Birth Chart

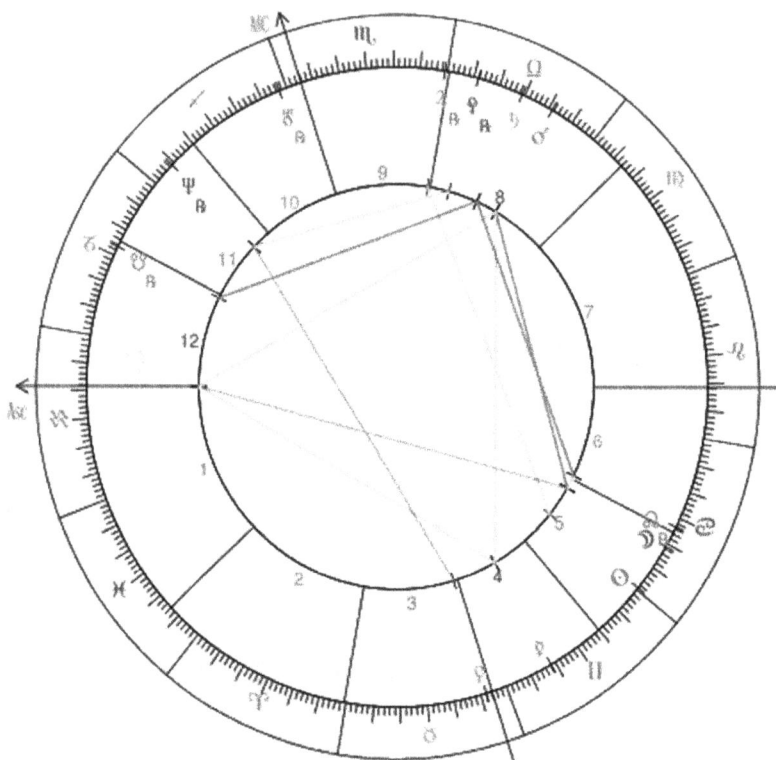

Birth Chart.
Morn, CC BY-SA 3.0 <https://creativecommons.org/licenses/by-sa/3.0>, via Wikimedia Commons https://commons.wikimedia.org/wiki/File:Natal_Chart_--_Adam.svg

Before anything else, you'll need a word processor or a pen and paper. You'll use those to work out the math for all the relevant elements of your chart. This will include:

- Your birth number
- Your destiny number
- Your personality number
- Your heart's desire or soul urge number

We've already gone over how to work these out and what each number means within each framework.

Benefits of Getting Your Numerology Chart

What are the benefits of getting a numerology chart? It's time to find out. Numerology is an ancient science that studies how numbers affect our lives. In numerology, every number has a meaning and a symbol associated with it, which are all interconnected. These associations bring about certain personality traits or offer insights into the events of your life.

Since numerology predicts events based solely on your name and the date and time of your birth, it can answer questions you may have about your future and help you make important decisions in life that will lead to happiness. It can help you better understand yourself and the people in your life. It can also show you how to work on relationships, avoid bad habits, make career changes, or become the best version of yourself. A Chaldean numerology chart may be for you if you're looking for meaning in numbers and a better understanding of your place in life.

The process of interpreting charts can be done with several specific methods to find the meanings of numbers. There are many different methods and techniques that numerologists use.

Symbol Analysis: In this method of numerology, symbols are given to numbers based on their characteristics. The number's symbol usually represents an important concept or quality about the number. For example, if your birthday is July 11th, you'll have the number 2 as your symbol (1 + 1 = 2).

Number Interaction: In this method, the numbers that make up an individual's chart are compared and analyzed. The purpose of this is to identify a relationship between each number and the other numbers on the chart. The relationships could be positive or negative or a combination of both.

Yearly Cycle: The hierarchy of the numbers varies from year to year. This is because every year has its own numerical energies. For example, 5 is considered lucky from 1986 to 1995 but unlucky from 1996 to 2005, and vice versa for years after 2005 (until 2026). Because of this, you should use caution when interpreting your chart for years that are more than six years apart (for example, you should use caution when interpreting your chart if your birthday is 1990 or 1982). This method can also be used to identify good or bad periods in an individual's life or family history due to a number's performance during a specific year.

Calculation: The next method of interpreting a chart involves adding up all the numbers in the individual's birth date (excluding month and day) and birth year. These two numbers are then compared to characteristics corresponding to the numerical sum. The actual mathematical process can be determined by typing in the birth date, year, and numbers that make up your name into a Numerology calculator -- many of which you can find online for free. You can also work out the answers manually if you prefer.

Working with Your Name

Let's begin with the birth name or given name. Remember, unlike Pythagorean numerology, you have the freedom to use whatever name you want. This is a good thing because if you notice your birth name has challenging energies, you can always change your name to something that feels better to you. You'd be shocked and amazed at how people's lives changed for the better the moment they chose to switch names. Your name is so important when it comes to building your chart because it carries the essence of who you are along with your birth date. It will show you why you act and think the way you do. Once you've got your name, you can then work with the information given in this book to write out the things that apply to the numerological value of your name. Remember, when working out any number connected to your name, you must assign the letter Y its proper position as either a vowel or a consonant. For instance, if your name is Yolanda, in this case, the letter Y is a consonant. If your name's Andy, it's a vowel because it isn't starting the word but ending it.

Working with Your Birth Date

Your birth date can also tell you about who you are. When you're crafting your chart, you should always set it in this format: MM-DD-YYYY. So, say you were born on the 24th of March 1991. You would write that out as 03-24-1991. Also, remember that unless you want to get the compound meaning of your numbers, whether birth or something else, you're to reduce the number to a single digit.

Now that you've got both your name and date of birth in hand, filling out your chart becomes easy. We've already talked about how to make these calculations. Still, because this is a reference chapter, we're going to do a quick recap of how to work out each one so that you can accurately fill out your chart with ease without having to flip back and forth between pages.

For your convenience, here's the Chaldean numerology table of values again:

1 2 3 4 5 6 7 8

A B G D E U O F

Q R C M H V Z P

Y K L T N W

I S X

J

For Your Compound Numbers: Add the values of your name until you get a two-digit answer. Do the same thing for your birth date. If you don't get a compound number, that's fine.

For Your Principal or Root Numbers (The Ones with Single Digits): Simply reduce everything until you get a single number from 1 to 8. If the answer you get is a 9, then you must look at the compound numbers that, when added together, would give you 9: for instance, 18, 27, 36, and so on.

For Your Destiny Number: Add up all the numbers that make up your name in their entirety. For Pythagorean numerology, that would be the name on your documents like your birth certificate. For Chaldean numerology, please work with your present assigned name (which technically would be on your documents anyway).

For Your Heart's Desire Number: You're only to add the values of every vowel in your name. Once more, remember the rule of Y.

For Your Personality Profile Number: Add all the consonants in your name. Once more, remember the rule of Y.

Your Birthdate Number: Add up all the numbers on your birthday, including month, year, and day. Then you'll know what to do if you get a compound number or a root number.

Expression Planes

This is the process of combining all the important numbers in your chart, which we've already outlined in the previous section. It's really easy to determine this because all you're doing is adding every one of these numbers together. For instance, let's assume that your destiny number is

8, your heart's desire number is 3, your personality number is 7, and your birthdate number is 6. Adding all of these together would give you 24, which can be reduced to 6.

What does this aspect of the numerology chart tell you exactly? It shows you the many layers of yourself and how you interact with others around you. You'll learn the way people see you, and it also combines their perception of you with the real reason you're here on this earth and whatever it is you want the most out of life. It's also worth taking note of your plane of expression because within it is where you'll find enlightenment on why you struggle and what could be holding you back. For instance, you may be shocked to find out that your desire to project yourself as someone different from who you really are is the only thing holding you back from success and attaining your goals and dreams.

What about Your Attainment Number?

This number is very important, and it is just a principal digit on your chart. What does it represent? It is the essence of your soul. You may change clothes, switch locations, change names, start a new career, or whatever, but your soul remains eternally unchanged. So, the attainment number is who you really are in spirit. Since all things flow from spirit, it is only wise to know what this number is and work with it mindfully so that you never have to worry about being off your path, and you'll attain a certain level of ease, flow, and acceptance of where you are in life. Some people say you should never accept anything you don't want or like, but the secret is that this is the first step towards changing it for the better. When you allow yourself to see the truth about your personal existence, you may be swamped with limitations, but your eyes will finally be open to the tools and resources around you that you can use to make the very best of it. Here's a shocker: when you do this, you might find that what you thought you wanted isn't exactly what you wanted or needed and that you quite like this new, more authentic, true version of yourself fueled and approved by your spirit.

Your attainment number is the very blueprint of your whole life, and the lives before this one and the lives that will come after. This number cuts through all the fluff and will show you as you really are, with no added frills. How do you calculate this number? All you have to do is add your destiny number and heart's desire number together, and the total should tell you all you need to know. Remember, the result should not be a compound number, so reduce it to a single digit — unless that's a 9, then you can work with the compound meanings assigned to figures that add up to 9.

A Sample Chart

Let's assume we're doing a chart for someone named Janet Bethany Archer, and she was born October 3, 1995.

JANET BETHANY ARCHER, 10–03–1995.

Destiny Number: 1 + 1 + 5 + 5 + 4 (JANET) + 2 + 5 + 4 + 5 + 1 + 5 + 1 (BETHANY) + 1 + 2 + 3 + 5 + 5 + 2 = 57.

Compound Number: 57.

Root Number: 5 + 7 = 12; 1 + 2 = 3

Heart's Desire Number: A, E, E, A, Y, A, E = 1 + 5 + 5 + 1 + 1 + 1 + 5 = 19

Compound Number: 19

Root Number: 1 + 9 = 10; 1 + 0 = 1

Personality Profile Number: J, N, T, B, T, H, N, R, C, H, R = 1 + 5 + 4 + 2 + 4 + 5 + 5 + 2 + 3 + 5 + 2 = 38

Compound Number: 38

Root Number: 3 + 8 = 11; 1 + 1 = 2

Birthdate Number: 1 + 0 + 0 + 3 + 1 + 9 + 9 + 5 = 28

Compound Number: 28

Root Number: 2 + 8 = 10; 1 + 0 = 1

Attainment Number: 4 (Destiny number 3, heart's desire number 1. 3 + 1 = 4.)

Destiny: 3. Entertainer, an entrepreneur who will flourish in creative work.

Heart's Desire: 1. Leadership and command. She will do well starting her own business or projects.

Personality Profile: 2. Diplomat, excellent partner. Possesses tact. Ability to switch between sensitive and insensitive, thoughtful and irrational.

Birthdate Number: 1. Born leader. Original. Massive will. Innovator. Bossy. Lacking intact.

Attainment Number: 4. Builder, disciplined, responsible, structured.

This was just an example of what a chart could look like, but you can actually go into many further details if you want to. For instance, we know that Janet is very creative. Instead of working for someone or for an organization where she may not be valued or allowed to flourish as she could, she would be much better off working on her own thing, striking off on her own. She could also do well as a partner, but it's more likely that she will find fulfillment working on her own. The same thing applies when it comes to relationships and friendships. She is very likely the sort of person who will strike up a conversation first or make the first move. This is a good thing for her, provided it's with the right people.

Possessing two number 1s means she must be careful about trampling on other people's opinions and feelings because she's the boss or because she senses she's right. This could also translate to her love life, where there may be times her partner attempts to get through to her on a difficult subject, but she doesn't listen because her mind's made up about what she would rather do. She would do very well with someone who has a predominance of 2 energy in their chart.

Whatever Janet wants to accomplish in life, she cannot afford to act without planning. She is naturally gifted at making things happen, provided she has a blueprint or plan to help her attain her goals in an orderly fashion, as she thrives when there's structure. She will not do well in environments where the rules aren't clear.

Chapter 9: Compatibility Numbers

Did you know that working with Chaldean numerology can help you figure out the people you're compatible with in terms of friendship and romance? Sure, there are other systems you could work with to help you with this, astrology being one of the more popular ones, but with numerology, you'll find interestingly accurate results. This is because numbers are in everything, and they carry unmistakable frequencies.

Chaldean numerology can tell who you're compatible with.

Before we get into the subject of compatibility, please do not assume that just because someone isn't compatible, you could never work things out with them. It's absolutely not the case because anyone could get along with anyone else as long as both people decide to work through their issues instead of being one of those obnoxious people who say, "Oh, I never date anyone who's a number 5" or something like that. You may encounter more issues than usual with the incompatible numbers, but that doesn't mean you can't make it work. After all, love is about growing.

Working Out Compatibility

To figure out whether or not someone is compatible with you, you want to work with their destiny number, personality profile number, and the Heart's Desire number. Comparing these numbers with one another is a great way to see if you and the other person will be a good fit in terms of numerology. You can tell whether you're always going to be engaged in arguments or if you'll get along just fine.

Numerology can tell you whether or not you're built to last, but if you need to ask that question in the first place, you might want to ask yourself why you're curious about that. Could it be that you're not really invested in the relationship? Could the fear of commitment be bothering you? Could it be that you need to work through some serious trust issues? There's nothing wrong with checking your compatibility, but you should always be sure of your reasons. It's much better to check with the mindset of wanting to make sure that things work out because you want to really understand the other person and truly grow together.

Relationships with a non-compatible number aren't doomed from the start. In fact, some of the best friendships and relationships began with a bit of fire and brimstone. All you're trying to do right now is to take a look at the destiny, personality, and heart's desire numbers for each of you. Now we'll check out the various combinations and see how they work together.

1 and 1

This combination is potent – as long as the two parties can find it within themselves to cede control to the other every now and then. If you're in this friendship or relationship, you need to know that you both have strong ambitions, and this could lead to some friction between you which could end up becoming resentment much later on. However, when you choose to be respectful of each other and allow each other to have a turn at holding the reins, you'll both be able to be frank with each other about your needs. Your partnership will become one where neither person is ever unsure or uncertain about what the other needs. The way for this to work out is through communication. If you don't communicate with each other, the magic you seek will never happen, and you're often going to lock heads. Be mindful of that.

1 and 2

This relationship or friendship is full of love and warmth, but despite all that, it may not be enough for either of you. The thing is that the 2 requires the reassurance of 1, and 1 is often more concerned with their ambition than anything else. If 1 regards the relationship as a key part of their goals, it will be great. That way, it's more than likely that things will work out. 1 loves to be in charge, while 2 are happy to lend emotional support, and this is a lovely dynamic to have with bosses and employees, parents and children, and so on. You're both likely to do well together as long as no one tries to take over the other person's duties or roles.

1 and 3

A thrilling and glorious combination with lots of stimulation. This is a wonderful relationship that brings out the best in you. You're both independent and self-sufficient; this is a great combination for people who want to hang out with one person all the time. You'll also be interested in one another's pasts because this is an understanding and compassionate combination of soul urges. This could be troublesome if your opinions clash too much, but you can function well together when you communicate well.

1 and 4

You're both sensitive and caring, but it doesn't go beyond that since the 1 and 4 combination has already brought up enough messy stuff. Your relationship is likely to be characterized by a lot of love and a lot of fighting. Neither of you'll find another person as loyal as the other, so chances are you'll continue to work through your issues and do your best to keep this going. However, it doesn't look like this will last forever since there's just too much sadness in it all.

1 and 5

This is a strong combination for those who want to take things slowly and live their lives one day at a time. You might be tempted to over-analyze everything, but that's what you're trying to do anyway, so it's no surprise that you're drawn together in deeper ways than the average relationship. However, you'll run into trouble when either of you feels that the other is moving too slowly.

1 and 6

This is a great combination for people looking for something stable. You're both very nurturing and loving towards one another, so it's no wonder that you'd be drawn together. The problem here is that the two of you are both very protective in nature but not so good at communicating how you feel. This can make your relationship appear stagnant, even though it's actually progressing just fine. You'll need to remember that communication is a two-way street to make things work.

1 and 7

This is a good combination, but not quite great. You're both independent, loving people who don't feel the need to do things halfway. That's the problem, though, because you're both too stubborn and set in your own ways to realize it. You could absolutely have a great relationship if you decided to learn how to communicate more effectively so that you could compromise and walk through the tunnel of change.

1 and 8

You're intense and emotional with each other, which could be misconstrued as a problem since this is an overwhelming combination for others. You're both capable of being too domineering, but you sense that about each other, so you'll probably be able to keep things measured and under control. That said, there have been times when this combination works out beautifully, with lots of love and support from both parties.

1 and 9

You're two extremely loyal people with lots of love to give in this relationship. The only problem is that neither of you is really good at being direct nor keeping your feelings to yourself. You might want to work on that if you want your relationship to last.

2 and 2

No one understands a 2 better than another 2. You'll both do wonderfully well together because you're so supportive of each other. You're both excellent at listening, and the fact that each person is willing to show their emotions and wear their heart on their sleeve will encourage the other person to do more of the same. This is a very nurturing relationship and could be a lifelong, beautiful thing.

2 and 3

This is a vigorous combination, with the two of you being able to bounce off of each other and create something very new and exciting.

You're both fantastic at speaking your minds and very open to hearing what the other has to say. This is a wonderful relationship for people who do well as friends first and partners second. There's nothing wrong with that dynamic, but you have to be careful not to lose yourself in this relationship since it can sometimes be difficult to see where one person ends and the other begins. Being able to communicate with someone who understands your points of view can be a real pleasure, especially when it comes to discussing a lot of different ideas with someone who's not afraid to try them out. You're both very creative, and you understand that you need to be given a chance to share your ideas. The tricky part is that you're both extremely direct in showing your emotions and expressing yourself.

2 and 4

You're both creative and intelligent, but your personalities are too alike to work well together. You're the type of person who wants to sit down, talk things out and then move forward. But you can't both do that at once, so there's bound to be a lot of hesitancy between you two until you decide which one of you'll take the reins when it comes to making decisions. It could be a solid relationship if it works out, but otherwise, it might feel more like a friendship than a romantic partnership.

2 and 5

This is an incredible combination of two genuinely sensitive people who are interested in finding out more about themselves and each other as they grow together. You both love to learn, and you're both very creative but with a natural understanding of what it's like to be human. This relationship could have really interesting ups and downs, but it could be really amazing when it works out.

2 and 6

You're both very loyal people who find yourselves drawn to one another for emotional reasons, so you'll do your best to stay together. You can only go as far as the other person pushes you, though, which means that this will rely heavily on communication for anything real to happen between the two of you. The good news is that you're both honest with each other, even if that means telling the truth when it hurts.

2 and 7

You're both extremely creative people who will enjoy the chance to spend time together. You're both very sensitive, and you'll feed off of one another's emotions, which could be overwhelming at times. This is especially true if you're not as daring with each other as you are with others. You can't let your relationship make you lazy, but on the other hand, it will probably encourage you to do more cool stuff together than either of you would do on your own.

2 and 8

There's no denying that this combination between two extremely independent people can be a bit explosive in nature when things don't go well. But it can be really enjoyable when you both have similar mindsets and wear your emotions on your sleeves. You'll be able to learn a lot from one another, no matter what kind of relationship you're trying to establish.

2 and 9

You're both very supportive people who understand and accept each other's needs. However, sometimes the problem is that neither one of you is the type of person to tell others about the things bothering them. You could learn a lot from this relationship if you decide it's time for communication to take center stage in your daily life.

3 and 3

You're both flexible people who can have conflicting wants and needs, which makes things tricky at times. You're also good at working out your differences together and solving them, so this might not be so bad after all. It helps that you can communicate well with one another, even if it does make the other feel a little needy from time to time. The biggest problem is that you're both highly independent people, so anything you do together will have to be a joint decision. Otherwise, things could get really complicated.

3 and 4

Independent people can have conflicting desires. This is especially true for this combination, which can lead to a lot of fighting if the two of you don't work on your communications skills. But if you can manage to talk things out and resolve any issues, this could be a great pairing. The two of you are very honest with each other and with yourselves. You'll never have to worry about being lied to or having your partner turn into someone you don't recognize. This is a very supportive combination because both of you are very willing to look at all aspects of your lives with openness and honesty before making any decisions.

3 and 5

You both want the same things out of life, and you're both naturally supportive people, so that's a great start. But you're also really sensitive types who will hurt each other's feelings from time to time if you aren't careful about how you approach one another. You can make this work by having discussions with each other about what more involvement in your relationship could feel like. But if you're not careful, this combination could be frustrating for one or both of you.

3 and 6

You're both conscientious people who definitely want to make something out of their lives. You can get along well because you've got similar interests and ideas about things, but there's a bit of a problem with romance. You both like being pampered by your partners and having the chance to relax together on occasion. This will challenge the two of you at times, especially if you run into old habits that don't work well together. It's definitely worth a try, though, as you both enjoy being each other's biggest supporters.

3 and 7

You're both very independent people who like to make their own decisions, so there can be some frustration in this pairing since you don't always agree on the same things. You're both very creative people, but things will get pretty tense if you are more advanced or the other is stuck in your ways. You're a little too independent for each other, which hinders any potential for a romantic relationship between you.

3 and 8

You value your freedom, which can cause some major tension between you if you're not careful. The easiest solution to this is for the two of you to respect one another's freedom, even if it means that neither one of you'll ever get exactly what you want out of this relationship. You're both going to have a hard time letting go and trusting each other, so experiments with fidelity will have to be completely open and agreed upon in advance.

3 and 9

You share a lot in common regarding empathy, sensitivity, and compassion. But there's a big problem with this combination: you really don't like to talk about emotions. You both want people who see the world through rose-colored glasses and don't let on that anything is bothering them, even if it isn't what you want to hear. This can make things tough for you because you're too sensitive to the other's quirks and habits.

4 and 4

You're essentially perfect for each other because this relationship will give you the chance to work out any issues holding back your compatibility. You've got fairly similar personalities, which means some things can only be improved upon by spending more time together. This is definitely a good thing because you both want to do the same things in life, but you're also really independent people who like to make their own decisions. A little compromise every once in a while is necessary.

4 and 5

You're both hardworking people who have similar ideas and interests, so there's no need for this relationship to turn into a losing battle. But when it comes down to the basic needs of human connection, there are some problems here. Both of you are very focused on your own needs and your own desires, which means that unless either one of you can see beyond themselves at times, then things will get tense and uncomfortable from time to time.

4 and 6

You're both very passionate people who like to enjoy life to the fullest. This would be a good combination if you could spend more time together, but as with most of these combos, that's only going to happen when you really push yourself together and make a strong effort. You've got similar interests, some of which are similar attitudes in life. There are just some basic differences here that prevent this from becoming anything more than a forced partnership.

4 and 7

You're both very sensitive people who are very easily wounded by other people's actions. This leads to a lot of resentment and jealousy, but this relationship has the potential to be very effective for the two of you because you're both going to get along well enough when you're not feeling any sort of pain. You may feel like you're getting ripped off more than anyone else, but there's no doubt that you're both very hardworking individuals who deserve to be taken care of and appreciated by others.

4 and 8

You've got a lot in common with one another regarding your values and beliefs, which is why this pair should work out well if you can get beyond some basic unresolved issues. The big problem here is that you both place very high expectations on one another, which can lead to a lot of tension between the two of you in the future. But as long as you're willing to work together on your issues, then this is a good combination for one another.

4 and 9

You're both very emotional people who feel everything deeply and need plenty of time to yourself to process your thoughts and feelings. This could be a good thing if you could learn how to better share yourself with others, of course, with the help of each other. There's an almost innate feeling of understanding between the two of you that makes it easy for you to get along with each other in all sorts of situations outside of just romance.

5 and 5

You're both very independent people who like to do things on your own terms, and you're both looking for someone who's just as independent. The problem with this pairing is that you're both expecting the other person to be everything to you, which can be overwhelming for you. You have a lot in common and many things that make you feel frustrated with one another. You need a break from one another on occasion, but as long as neither of you gives up, it can still be good between the two of you.

5 and 6

You're both hardworking individuals who are compatible with one another when it comes to your goals in life and even in enjoying life. You're both isolated in your own little worlds, which is good if you see each other as your only hope. But what happens when those worlds can't get along with each other? The trouble between the two of you'll be well worth it if there's enough fun to be had in the process. This can be tough at times, but keep pushing forward, and one day, things will get better.

5 and 7

You're both very loyal and devoted to your jobs and would like to spend more time together with the other person. This can be a good thing, but it's also going to be relatively difficult to build an actual relationship with each other because you both tend to have very different ideas of how things should be done. You have some things in common, but you'll also have many things that make you feel like you're not being understood or valued, leading to resentment at times.

5 and 8

You're both very independent people who also care about ensuring that everyone around you has everything they need in life. You've got similar ideas about what's best for the world and your behavior towards other people, which is a promising start for this relationship. But the main problem here is that you both have such high expectations of each other, which can lead to a lot of strain between you. This doesn't have to be the case, but it depends on your dedication to making this work for your family and yourself.

5 and 9

You're both very passionate people with many things in common and some things that will divide you from one another. You both want to make sure that your family is safe from harm, but you each have different ways of going about doing it. The problem with getting along with each other comes down to these differences in opinions. If you could get past the differences, you could make this relationship into a very strong union.

6 and 6

There's a lot of good stuff going on with this pairing, but unfortunately, most of it is kept hidden from the world because you're both so isolated from one another by your own insecurities. This can lead to some conflicts because neither of you wants to deal with your insecurities, and it just comes out as anger towards one another. You both share some of the same goals in life but think very differently about bringing them to pass. This will be a difficult pairing that requires more communication than most other combinations.

6 and 7

You're both very hard-working people who know exactly how to enjoy your time together. There's a lot of good stuff happening here because you both have similar ideas about life in general, but there's an underlying difference between the two of you, which will lead to a lot of frustration between the two of you. You've got some deep-seated issues that will eventually rise to the surface, and when they do, things will get difficult enough for you that it will be hard for either one of you to make it work long-term.

6 and 8

You're both very attentive and sensitive people who are willing to do whatever it takes to ensure that you're getting all the care and attention you need, making you very compatible. You have some deep-seated issues that will eventually lead to problems in your relationship. Still, there's enough good stuff going on here that it can work for the two of you if your two personalities could get past some of their differences.

6 and 9

You learn from each other and can take a lot of positives away from your relationship, which is why you both can make it work even through tough times. You're both more than willing to take on the responsibility of your family, and you're both very attractive people who are good at what you do. The biggest problem with this pairing is that neither of you'll admit that there's a problem between you, which will stop this relationship from growing into something bigger.

7 and 7

You're both very independent people who like to take things slow and just enjoy the journey along the way, which goes a long way towards your compatibility with one another. You're both very loyal people who are willing to forgive mistakes that others make because it's something that you don't like holding onto for too long. You both want to be happy above all else, and there's a lot of passion between you. This pairing has the potential to make things work for a long time, which is what you're both going to need from each other to keep your relationship grounded in reality.

7 and 8

You're both very independent people who have a lot of respect for yourself and each other, which will make it easy for the two of you to get along with one another. The main issue here is that you're both used to doing things on your own terms, and neither one of you wants to give up that independence, at least not yet. There's a lot of good stuff happening here, and the two of you can go a long way towards making it work if you want to, but there are also a lot of risks involved in how you two handle one another.

7 and 9

There's a lot of passion in this relationship because you're both very observant people who are good at reading each other. This is promising because it gives both of you plenty of ways to solve problems without resorting to getting angry. You're both very patient people who like taking things slow, which is great because it gives the two of you a chance to build up a solid foundation for your relationship. You both want to make sure that everyone around you is happy, but you have different ways of doing it.

8 and 8

You're both independent people who have a very sensible and realistic way of looking at life, which will make the two of you a good team in many situations. The main problem with this relationship is that neither one of you has any idea how to accept help from the other to get things done. It's not going to work out for the two of you because neither one of you is willing to open up and admit that they're capable of needing help from someone else. You're both very loyal people who are willing to forgive each other for their mistakes, but there are too many things about each other that you're unwilling to accept.

8 and 9

This is an interesting pairing because it will take a lot of effort on both of your parts to make it work. You're both very independent people who don't like being far away from one another, which can cause some problems between the two of you because neither one of you is very affectionate towards the other in social situations. You have similar objectives in life but different approaches. This is promising because it gives the two of you a chance to try something different and see if it works, but there are a lot of risks involved here as well because you both have very strong personalities that will get in the way of making your relationship work.

9 and 9

This is an easy pairing because the two of you are very good at understanding and respecting one another's point of view. You're both independent people who are usually happy to do things in a way that fits your own schedule and conditions. There's not a lot of room for growth in this relationship because you're both used to doing the same things in life that the other is doing, which means that things won't get any better between the two of you. This will be a difficult pairing because you both have so much respect for each other but don't know how to deal with things.

Chapter 10: Calculate the Vibrational Value of Everything

In this chapter, you'll learn how numerology can help you in your life. Everything has a vibrational value in the form of its own unique numbers, including places, people, animals, dates for occasions, and so much more. There's much to be gained from using numerology to advance in life, as it can help you see where your strengths and weaknesses lie, help you deal with the challenges that will come your way with a sense of ease and grace, and see better ways to connect with spirit in your life, and lots more. Working with numbers to hack the game of life is very easy. Let's go over how numerology can be a game-changer for you. Let's explore how you can apply numerology to your daily life.

Make Investment Decisions

By using numerology in your investment decisions, you'll be able to make wise choices about how and where you invest in the future. You see, whether you're investing in the stock market, real estate deals, cryptocurrencies, or whatever else, every investment is a gamble of some sort — and you can increase your odds of making a profit if you use the wisdom that comes with numerology. How? By harmonizing what you're working with numerology.

Numerology can guide you with investment decisions.
https://unsplash.com/photos/jpqyfK7GB4w

If you're planning on investing in the stock market, for instance, it makes sense to calculate the energy of all of the numbers associated with that particular market — be it financial markets or otherwise. After that, you can decide whether or not it feels right to invest. The beauty of doing this is that it takes you out of the realm of "gut feeling" and into a more rational and analytical framework where your mind is open to making decisions based on facts, not on what's "feeling good." Use numerology for all your investment decisions to make wise choices about how and where you invest your hard-earned money.

Enhance Your Relationship Compatibility

Relationships are hard work when they're new. In fact, they're often very hard work. But you can use numerology to learn when your relationship is in sync with other people. Do you have a partner that you're not compatible with? Using numerology, you'll be able to see what the core issues are between you two. This will also tell you how much time and energy it will take to remedy those issues. It's not meant to be a depressing revelation either — it's just a useful way to find out where things are at in your relationship so that the two of you can start making changes together. You see, relationships don't remain stagnant forever — they grow and develop over time, just like everything else in life. You and your partner will want to do what you can to help one another grow, no? Then why wouldn't you want to use numerology — not just for the two of you, but for all your other relationships as well?

Enhance Your Spiritual Development

You see, numerology is a compass that points the way to where we want to go. So, you don't need any special instruction for it to work for you. It simply works because everything has a vibration — including numbers. It's about realizing the connection between you, your world, and all the other worlds which intermingle with your own. When you know how to interpret those connections, you'll be able to make sense of things in an interesting and very useful way. Everything in life is a puzzle — and numerology is one of many tools that will help you solve that puzzle. It provides valuable insights into life and into yourself.

Make Changes in Your Life

I think it's safe to say that every great life change starts with a decision. When you use numerology to make that decision, you'll get a lot more out of it in the long run. Numerology can help you realize what kind of person you truly are — it can show you strengths and weaknesses and talents and challenges. Life is a journey, and you're changing every step of the way. But how often do we make those changes without giving them a second thought? Probably not very often at all. So, what about using numerology to make a change in your life? If numerology works for everything else around you, then why not use it as a way to bring about change in your life too? It makes sense, doesn't it? The more you understand yourself and the more you can interpret what's going on around you, the happier and better off you'll be. As you learn to use numerology, everything starts to make more sense — it's as simple as that!

Help You Raise Your Kids

You already have a lot on your plate as parents. Between keeping your household running and raising your kids, there's a lot to do. But numerology can help you cope better with it all. When you're dealing with children and their day-to-day lives, you don't have time to second guess yourself — every decision is important and has long-term ramifications. So, I recommend that you use numerology to narrow down your options when making these decisions — it'll keep you grounded in reality so that your intuition is both serviced and kept intact at all times. Let's say that one of the kids keeps getting into arguments with another child at school.

Before you know it, the two kids are fighting each other to the point where they're really hurting one another. What do you do then? Do you play the "he said, she said" game? Or do you use numerology to decide how to handle this problem — especially since it's become something that is causing your child more stress than they need?

If, instead of taking on all of these challenges, both children could learn that they're not having an argument — that they're actually making up a story — then what would that benefit be for them? Among other things, you'd be removing a lot of unnecessary energy from your home. One of the best things you can do to help your kids grow up to be healthy, happy adults is to teach them how to use numerology. You see, understanding numerology is a very valuable life skill — it's all about understanding how everything in the universe works and how numbers influence everything that happens in our world. When you can make sense of how numbers work and why they do — and when you do it with love and respect — then you're helping your kids grow up into self-aware and determined adults.

Use It to Identify the Best Business Partners

Another way numerology can help you is by identifying the best business partners. Finding good business partnerships is a very tricky thing. There's a lot to say about having the right partnership to help you advance in your career and drive profits. But how do you know whether or not a business partner will help you and how can you use numerology to figure out if they're right for you? The key is to look at the energy behind their name — there's something called numerology compatibility, which is based on the energy behind each individual person's name. Use that energy as a barometer for your partnership and for figuring out if it'll be successful or not. It takes the guesswork out of business partnerships. Every businessman wants to know that he's working with someone who'll get the job done — and nothing beats that feeling of doing business with someone who understands what it is you're all about. When you use numerology, you'll be able to work in harmony with another person, which means increased chances of success.

Figure Out Your Career Goals

You often don't know your career goals when you're young. As a result, you make choices that do not match what really matters to you. Young people make this very common mistake — so common, in fact, that the media commonly uses it to sell their products. This is a big mistake because we tend to work harder than necessary when we have career goals that are not aligned with our core values. Sometimes we work so hard that it becomes counterproductive — sometimes too hard even to enjoy what we're doing. As part of your mission in life, use numerology as your guide to work towards these goals and objectives. It's hard to know what you want in life when you're young. But numerology can help you figure out your career goals — and it doesn't matter if those goals are big or small. After all, knowing what you want gives your life direction. Having this kind of direction in your life is very important, no?

Use It to Make Wise Financial Decisions

If you're concerned about financial decisions, then it makes sense to learn more about numerology. After all, nothing has a better track record than how well it can help us in everything from investing to making financial decisions. In fact, numerology is one of the most reliable ways to make wise financial choices.

Whether you're a big spender or a little frugal, numerology can help you make wise financial decisions. When you use numerology, you'll see that there is no such thing as coincidence — and that everything has a reason. In our world, money makes the world go round. Numerology enables us to interpret the energy of numbers to make wiser financial choices — and that's something everyone should know how to do.

Make Good Decisions in General

Making good decisions is similar to making wise financial choices — it's all about doing your research and making sure that the decision matches your goals, values, and long-term plans. With numerology as your compass, you have all the information you need at your disposal to make the best decision possible.

Use It to Interpret Dreams

You probably wonder about your dreams every now and then. Why would anyone ask a question like that when they've already dreamed it? Why wouldn't they just leave well enough alone? Why ask something they already know the answer to, right? But when you use numerology, you'll be able to make sense of your dreams and why you have them. You can use numerology to figure out the meaning of the symbols that stuck out to you the most in the dream, or you could use it for the names of the people you saw. You can do the same thing for the locations you dream of or if you have one of those dreams where a certain word jumps out at you.

Grow a Healthy Family

If you have children, you know that most parents want nothing more than for their children to feel connected — to everything — and for them to grow into healthy, happy adults. Using numerology will help you build upon your emotional bond with your children — making it stronger than ever before. This can help you not just with your kids but also with your entire family.

Understand What Makes People Tick

If you don't know why people act the way they do, then you'll never be able to understand what makes them tick. Numerology enables you to understand this — and it's easier than you think. Why? Because everything has a vibration — everything has a meaning. When you know how to interpret that meaning, you'll start to understand how people operate. It's not that difficult at all — and once you start doing it, you'll find yourself with all kinds of answers about others around the world too.

Determine If Someone Is Worthy of Your Time — or Not

We often don't know whether or not someone is worth our time until we've sat down with them one on one for a while. But why waste all of that effort when there's an easier way? Instead of doing this, use numerology to figure out if they're worth talking to in the first place.

Numerology Can Help You with Your Health

Did you know that numerology can help you figure out your health problems? When you use numerology, you'll be able to look at the numbers and understand which ones will play a part in your healing process. Everything that happens in our lives does so for a reason. When we can see past the reason we're given, we can offer ourselves the opportunity for change. Change is good — if it's under the right circumstances. You can use it to figure out the best foods for you to eat things that are compatible with you.

Numerology Can Help You Attain Spiritual Ascension

Numerology gives you the tools you need to attain spiritual ascension. It also gives you the information you need to understand the importance of ascension. Once you know what it is, it's easy to take action — and there's no better time than now. When we think about spiritual ascension, many of us might have difficulty believing that it's even possible. But if you use numerology to help you along in this process, you'll find yourself on the road to attaining spiritual ascension in no time at all. This is just one of those things that have the potential to help us grow. All you have to do is try to live in alignment with all the numbers that are relevant to you.

Can you think of any other ways you can work with numbers in your life? Whatever you can think of, numerology will help. It is such a wonderful tool that can help you fully live your life fully and reach your greatest potential.

Conclusion

You've finally come to the end of this book, and it's been quite a ride. Remember, the best thing you could possibly do is put what you've learned into practice, and don't stop with this book either. There is so much more you could learn about the subject.

A worthwhile practice is to meditate with these numbers in mind and see the impressions you get from each one. If you're helping others with their readings, you can also meditate with them in mind before you finally help them draw up a chart or explain what their challenges are and what they need to do to overcome them all.

Numbers have always been an intricate part of our lives, and it's such a fortunate thing that you have come to the place in your life where you now realize this and are actually taking action by reading this book. You must continue to contemplate what the numbers mean and take stock of your life from when you were born until this point in time to figure out how they've affected you all these years.

Remember, just because the numbers can be pretty accurate all the time doesn't mean that you're always doomed to experience the struggles connected to that number. You can actually overcome all things with some perseverance and faith in yourself. The numbers aren't meant to make you feel like you're being held captive to a fate you didn't sign up for; knowledge of numerology is meant to empower you and help you realize how much richer and more fulfilling your life could be if you followed the blueprint of your soul.

The deeper you dive into this topic, the more you'll discover, and the more it will be obvious to you that the Chaldeans knew *exactly* what they were doing when they came up with this system of divination. Don't be too hard on yourself for not being able to remember what every number stands for because you can and should take your time with this.

Part 2 Predictive Astrology

Unlock Ancient Secrets Surrounding Numbers, Divination, and Astrology

Introduction

Dear reader, it is no coincidence that you have stumbled upon this book. Everything in the universe works through divine timing. The circumstances that led you to this book were true, planned, and here you are, reading these words.

So why are you here? Is it mere curiosity? Are you a beginner astrologist who is seeking more astrological knowledge? Do you want to be a professional in the art of predictive Astrology?

Whatever your answer may be, you have come to the right place. This book does not shallowly discuss sun signs and some frivolous characteristics about who you are. On the contrary, this book digs deeply into the sacred knowledge of planets, signs, houses, placements, aspects, numerology, etc.

You are constantly affected by various ambiguous energies, and it is time for you to familiarize yourself with these mysterious influences. What do they want from you? How do they work? Why are they affecting you in that way? How do you interpret the planets' movements and understand them? It is time for you to know your position in the universe, your real identity, and your true path during this lifetime.

You might feel like the knowledge in this book is daunting, but there is no reason to worry. This book is perfectly designed for any beginner. Even if you do not know much about the topic, you'll find that everything here is easy to absorb and understand.

You will also get to practice what you have learned. You will find clear instructions to guide you and help you with astrological predictions. The more you practice what you have learned, the easier the learning process will be. You will become an avid Astrology student in no time, and you will be interpreting the movement of the planets with ease.

Chapter 1: Introduction to Predictive Astrology

Ancient Egyptians believed that the power of the New Year was instilled in them under the Draconis constellation.

https://www.pexels.com/photo/people-toasting-wine-glasses-3171837/

Astrology came into being with the emergence of man's great early civilizations. The earliest recording of Astrology is on the walls of Ancient Egyptian structures. They celebrated the New Year under the Draconis constellation, containing the North and South nodes. They believed that the power a New Year instills in them under this constellation is a connection with their inner consciousness.

Later, the Ancient Babylonians observed the celestial movements, and they noticed that every month there was a different constellation that showed up more prominently than others in the heavens. They also noted the movement of planets and placed special associations with their gods on these movements. They also believed that these movements carried messages.

These two civilizations paved the way for Western Astrology, which will be discussed in this book. The origins of Western Astrology came from the Ancient Greeks, who named the zodiac constellations. Based on their observations, they believed that every zodiac sign brought certain characteristics that would be more prominent. This is how Pisces became the emotional, dreamy sign, and Capricorn is the great taskmaster.

Like the Babylonians, the Romans named the planets after their gods, but theirs have stuck for good this time. To this day, the planets still have their Ancient Roman names.

Both the Greeks and Romans used Astrology as a form of divination. However, after the passing of the centuries, Astrology became more pseudo-science than actual science and less believed in. All that changed after Carl Jung released a book that discussed psycho-astrology, which connected Astrology and the human psyche. After that, Astrology took off once more and became the advanced astrology that we now know today.

Astrology works hand-in-hand with the Hermetic principle, "As above, so below." Each planet and sign carry different energies within them, and as they orbit together, they radiate energies that affect humankind. These energies are reflected in who you are, the environment that you were born in, and where your life is heading. Through Astrology, you can foresee upcoming events, your growth, and who you'll become.

Astrology is also strongly linked to Numerology, another pseudo-science that correlates numbers with life events and who you are as a person. The idea is that everyone has a life path, and whatever this number is, it is connected to one of the planets. This means that you are energetically connected to this planet through Numerology and Astrology.

In the coming chapters, you'll learn about the power of planets, what each represents, their effect on your everyday life, and their influence on you. You will also read about the different zodiac signs and houses you see in your birth chart. You will understand what they mean and represent.

After accumulating this astrological knowledge, you can glimpse into your past, present, and future. Your natal chart can thoroughly justify your past, explain your present, and give you the foresight to see into the future. Once you understand how to read your natal chart and, more importantly, how to use it, you can satisfy your curiosity and answer any question that has been endlessly roaming your mind.

Chapter 2: Planets and Their Numbers

Lately, social media has been flooded with Astro-talk about the "big three," the sun, moon, and rising sign. It has become so popular that the question now is, "What are your big three?" instead of, "What is your sun sign?"

There is no doubt that these astrological bodies hold the keys to our blueprints, but are they the only ones capable of that? Absolutely not. They are only a part of a greater puzzle. So, what about the rest? If you wonder about this, it is about time you see the full picture. Let us start with the sun.

The Sun

Glyph: ☉

The sun is the core of the solar system, and it is also the core of personality in the natal chart. It may not be a planet, but it is a powerful luminary body that shapes your identity and expresses who you are.

Its placement in the natal chart represents the struggle of individualization, ego, energy, authority figures, creative ability, and how humans take on challenges. This giant star has undeniable masculine energy. This is why it represents male figures, including the father.

However, how he is represented depends on which house the sun is in and the sign, and the kind of aspects it shares with the other planets.

It is common knowledge that the sun rules Leo, naturally affecting body parts like the upper back, thymus, heart, and spinal cord.

In numerology, number one represents leadership and independence, which is similar to the characteristics represented by the sun. No wonder number one is associated with the giant star.

It is also important to note that each luminary body and planet reacts differently under certain signs. When a planet is exalted under a specific sign, it gives its full power, and when it is in fall, its energy is barely felt.

Have you already guessed under which sign the sun is exalted? It is fair to assume that it is Leo, but it is Aries. The sun is domicile in Leo, meaning that it gives off a good amount of energy since it has rulership over this sign.

It is a detriment in Aquarius, however, so as an astrologer, you should expect the least amount of energy from it. It does not end here, though. This star is in fall in Libra, which is considered the weakest placement for it.

Even though there are other luminary bodies and planets that influence the lives of humans, the sun is one of the most vital celestial bodies to consider because of how much power it holds and how it shapes one's personality. This is why people always ask about sun signs more than anything else. They just want to know who you are at your core, and this is why astrologists check a client's sun sign before checking the rest.

Keywords:

- Individualization
- Ego
- Confidence
- Creative Expression
- Consciousness
- Vitality

Sign: Leo

House: 5th

Element: Fire

Symbol: Apollo's Shield

The Moon

Glyph: ☾

The moon has always been a mystical luminous body that humanity has held in high regard, and for a good reason. This shiny sphere influences emotions and governs intuition. You can easily feel its beautiful feminine energy when connecting with your emotions, listening to your intuition, and allowing yourself to be vulnerable. The moon also influences that nurturing side of you and your maternal instincts.

One of the key pieces of information about the moon is that it is exalted in Taurus, domicile in Cancer, detriment in Capricorn, and falls in Scorpio. It rules the stomach since it is a luminary body that is associated with maternity and nurture.

In numerology, the moon is associated with the number two. People who are represented by this number are sensitive, intuitive, emotional, caring, helpful, and highly affectionate. These characteristics mirror what the moon is all about, and it deeply resonates with number two natives.

Ruler of the fourth house and Cancer, the moon describes your relationship with your mother and could give you hints about your wife's essence. Depending on its placement in your natal chart, it could tell you how you deal with your emotional self, whether you tend to it or ignore it. To better understand this, you need to check which moon phase you were born under.

New moon folks are more enthusiastic when it comes to starting projects. Mirroring the new phase, they are usually bursting with fresh energy. However, this comes with a bit of naïveté and an inability to set real boundaries with themselves and those around them.

The second phase of the moon, also known as the waxing crescent, is growth-centered. Individuals born under this phase are naturally growth-oriented, progressive, and dynamic. These humans almost ooze vitality, and there is an undeniable freshness to them. Their drawback has to do with overcoming their past. They usually hold onto it for a long time and do not know how to let it go.

On the other hand, first-quarter people are driven to action by emotional turmoil most of the time. This internal conflict drives them to take action, leading them to project it onto others. They are generally fun to be around because they are exciting, and their drive is contagious. First quarters always know how to make things happen. They have an aggressive attitude toward taking on life, so they are often confused when their loved ones are not mirroring the same fiery frame of mind.

Much like the waxing crescent, Gibbous moon souls are growth-oriented. They seek enlightenment and education throughout their lives. They also have the drive to help their community or benefit society. It is usually illuminating to be around them because they are generally generous with their knowledge. However, they often find themselves bewildered when understanding themselves and the universe.

This leads us to the full moon. People born under this phase are full of potential and energy, almost mirroring the moon's bright light. Their enthusiasm and enlightenment are inspiring, and their flair is indisputable. They are often troubled emotionally and find themselves torn between their emotional and mental problems. However, this inner division is intensely felt, and most of their revelations break through this thick layer of inner conflict.

Born under the disseminating phase, these individuals are either spiritual or political messengers and are sometimes both. They are known for their sense of humor and their generosity with knowledge. Like a moth to a flame, they attract lovers, but that does not always secure a happy ending as far as their love lives go.

Similar to the first quarter, third quarter folks experience severe inner conflict. However, they internalize everything rather than project this stress onto others. They are very sure of themselves, especially regarding personal ideologies and principles. Flexibility is not in their dictionary, and they take criticism to heart. Their sentimentality softens their aloof demeanor, and their independence is often inspiring.

Known for their enlightened outlook, waning crescent individuals are in harmony with themselves and others. Other people's perspectives on life do not bother them in the slightest, and they are very much live and let live type of souls. They have a strong sense of self and sometimes wish others viewed life's simplicity the way they do.

Opposite the new moon, the dark moon is the last lunar phase. People born under this phase find themselves drawn to a life-altering destiny led by the universe. They are often prophetic and are willing to sacrifice themselves for a cause that could alter life for the better. They are a peculiar type of visionary, which is why others feel like dark moon folks are working for something far greater than themselves. Most of them are artistically talented, and their work stands out.

Keywords:

- Emotions
- Intuition
- Psychic abilities
- Security
- Nurture
- Mother
- Home
- Roots

Sign: Cancer

House: 4th

Element: Water

Symbol: A Crescent

Day of the Week: Monday

Number: 2

Moon's Nodes

Known as the Lunar Nodes, the North Node and the South Node are not planetary bodies in space but are rather calculated points opposite each other. They are calculated based on the relationship between the sun, moon, and time of birth.

The idea behind the nodes is that souls enter earth with overdeveloped and underdeveloped qualities from a past life. Revealing their karmic destination, the nodes act as a guide for humans leading them to their path.

The lunar nodes transit every 18 months, so remember that this is a universal sign to start working on different aspects of yourself every time it changes signs. Check what kind of aspects they have with your natal lunar nodes – if there are any.

They do not necessarily have a ruler like other signs but are ruled by whatever sign they fall under. An easy way to know which planet rules your moon nodes is by checking which planets rule the two signs that your lunar nodes occupy.

North Lunar Node

Glyph: ☊

Simply put, the North Node illuminates the path your soul is supposed to be following. You will not necessarily feel like you must follow this path, but you'll feel like you are being kindly nudged towards a certain road. Once you do follow this path, you'll feel like you belong. It will feel like your rightful place – as if you should have been there all along. Do not fret, though. If you feel lost, the general struggle is part of getting there.

South Lunar Node

Glyph: ☋

Opposite its lunar sister, the South Node shows what you are already good at. Think of it as a list of your natural gifts. These natural qualities will aid you in your life – but rely on them too much, and they become *a trap.*

Black Moon Lilith Glyph: ⚸

Similar to the Nodes, the black moon is not a floating body in space but refers to a point where the moon is farthest from the earth. This geometrical placement gets its name from the mythical Lilith. Believed to be Adam's first wife, she left him because she rejected his superiority. However, Lilith is seen as a liberated, rebellious, and autonomous woman. This sheds light on what the dark moon means in your natal chart.

Depending on its placement in your chart, Lilith reveals the nature of your shadow self and of who, profoundly, you are. It shows the presence or lack of inner authority, seductive powers, sensuality, and liberation. It also sheds light on your obsessive or self-destructive behavior and urges you to alter it.

The same logic applies when the dark moon is transiting. It stays nine months in one sign and then transits to another. When it lands in another sign and house, you are encouraged to think about the qualities that this placement represents to be aware of how you might behave during this period. Remember to check the dark moon's aspects with your natal Lilith.

Mercury

Glyph: ☿

Now that you know what influences your personality and emotions, it is time to introduce you to Mercury. This planet reveals the nature of the mind, how it works, and how it reacts and expresses itself. To better understand this, you might want to look at where your Mercury is. If it is in Sagittarius, you think like this sign; you have a brain full of curiosity. Your mind is more attuned to humanities, attracted to philosophy, and spends time thinking about the meaning of life. The same logic applies to any other sign and house.

Mercury is the closest planet to the sun, so if your sun sign is in Cancer, your Mercury might be in Leo. Having said that, locating this planet's placement should not be difficult. It generally either proceeds or precedes the sun.

Mercury represents communication, technology, transportation, self-expression, intellect, and general mental faculties in astrology. The way you talk, write, and go about these everyday activities are all influenced by this planet. It rules both energetic Gemini, disciplined Virgo, and the 3rd and 6th houses. It is exalted in Virgo, domicile in Gemini, detriment in Sagittarius, and fall in Pisces.

This celestial body also influences the respiration and nervous systems, so it is generally a good idea to take extra care of them when it is retrograde. Unfortunately, a lot of things can go wrong during a retrograde. This is why people tend to be suspicious, especially when astrologers advise them to never go under surgery or sign any contracts during this time of year.

The reasoning behind this suspicion is simple. This planet has a powerful influence over technology and our minds. Going under surgery could be dangerous because high-tech machines can go rogue, and maybe the doctor's mind will not be as focused. The same logic applies to contracts. You might be more inclined to skip over a few vital paragraphs or misinterpret a few words that could be detrimental to your career.

It is relatively easy to see why Mercury gets a bad rap, but it is essential to remember that most of the time, it only aids you and gives you the power to be focused and express yourself authentically.

Now that you have a good idea of what Mercury represents in astrology, it is time to look at it through numerology's lens. This planet has a connection with the number five. Generally, natives of this number embody typical Mercury characteristics. They are lively, intelligent, adventurous, and communicative.

Keywords:

- Mind
- Thinking
- Communication
- Intellect
- Technology
- Transportation
- Self-expression

Signs: Gemini & Virgo

Houses: 3rd & 6th

Elements: Air & Earth

Symbol: Mercury's Caduceus

Day of the Week: Wednesday

Number: 5

Venus

Glyph: ♀

The planet of love, Venus, is one of the most popular celestial bodies with new lovers. This planet heavily influences love lives, passing intimate relationships, and how people love and show affection. It also reveals some truths about sensuality, kinks, and female sexuality.

This love-centered planet rules both Libra and Taurus and the 2nd and 7th houses. It is exalted in Pisces, domicile in Libra and Taurus, detriment in Aries, and fall in Virgo. It rules kidneys, veins, and ovaries when it comes to bodily functions.

Venus' position is vital when it comes to relationships. Usually, clients ask about their partner's placement to learn more about their love language and how they like to be loved. The thing is, not everyone is aware of what they like in intimate relationships. These topics are murky for them, and they might not be aware of their style.

This is how Venus enlightens people. There are a lot of couples who like to compare their Venus sign with their partner's. This sheds a lot of light on how they can show affection in the relationship and be supportive harmoniously.

Other than human love lives, this planet also rules art. Think of music, paintings, photography, and any kind of activity that requires creativity. Venus rules this artistic side of you. It tells you what kind of art you like and how you prefer to express yourself creatively. This is why it also rules the beautifully balanced and artistic Libra.

Venus also rules finances, and anything related to money, bringing Taurus into its fold. If you want to know more about how money comes into your life, how fast or slow, and your relationship with it, then you might want to check which sign and house your Venus is in.

You might have noticed by now that this planet influences various aspects of one's life that relate to feelings. In other words, this planet co-rules emotions related to romantic relationships together with the moon.

This harmony between Venus and the moon indicates that they have high feminine energy and influence over female organs. However, this doesn't mean that men can not relate to either celestial body because all humankind has both feminine and masculine energy at the end of the day. It is safe to say that whether you are a woman or a man, either luminary body has a great influence over you, and it is vital to investigate what that means for you.

This planet has a harmonious relationship with the number six, and natives of this number mirror Venusian characteristics. It is easy to identify these people because of their sense of style and fashion. They love to be admired and know that they are wanted. They particularly enjoy luxurious items and tasty food and are fond of all kinds of art. It is easy for them to slip into a hedonistic lifestyle, and they are usually warned against this.

Keywords:

- Art
- Love life
- Affection
- Female Sexuality
- Sensuality
- Seduction
- Hedonism
- Female Energy
- Aesthetic beauty
- Relationships
- Finance

Signs: Libra and Taurus
House: 7th
Elements: Air & Earth
Symbol: Female Cross
Day of the Week: Friday
Number: 6

Mars

Glyph: ♂

In astrology, Mars and Venus are opposite sides of the same coin. An energetic planet, Mars is responsible for mankind's energy, survival, war, desire, assertion, and aggression. It also heavily influences the sexuality of men, sex life, and libido of both genders.

This planet rules Aries and the 1st house. It is also considered a sub-ruler for Scorpio. It is exalted in Virgo, domicile in Aries and Scorpio, detriment in Taurus and Libra, and fall in Cancer. It rules the bladder, male genitalia, and muscular system. Medical astrology says that it can inflict burns, cuts, sexually transmitted diseases, and accidents.

Many people look for their Mars placement because they want to know more about the kind of energy they have and where it is most expressed.

Some of them struggle with a lack of energy, and they want to know how they can kick start their Mars or how to work with what they have.

This usually happens when this planet is afflicted by another planet or aspect sucking its energy dry. Others feel like they have too much energy, and it turns into volatile or aggressive behavior, and they want to know how they can channel this energy in more healthy ways.

Others struggle with a malefic Mars in their birth chart. In astrology, malefic means to bring about bad fortune or influence ill behavior. It is associated with Mars and Saturn. This happens when the planet is placed in a sign that is either stifling its energy or heightens the more negative traits of Mars. When Mars' energy is suffocated, it results in anger issues and uncontrollable temper. Sometimes difficult aspects bring Mars' aggression and control to the surface, resulting in volatile relationships.

On a more positive note, there are ways to heal a malefic placement. You can start by finding out which sign and house your planet falls under. After you have done so, it is time to list all its aspects with other planets. Now that the easy part is over, you can start analyzing and seeing how Mars' malefic power manifests in your life.

It is important to note that astrology tells you what you were born with and how you can change it if need be. These characteristics can be changed if you work on them. There is a lot of healing to do, and that is exactly what malefic planets are guiding you to do.

Number 9 natives have high Mars energy. They can be competitive, energetic, and full of motivation. Some of them have high sex drives and often deal with anger issues. They can efficiently channel on either side of Mars. The key here is balance, and it is usually easy to establish once one finds out how to deal with all the abundant energy.

Keywords:
- Male Energy
- Drive
- Energy
- Self-preservation
- Libido
- Male Sexuality
- Aggression

- Rage
- Impulsiveness

Sign: Aries
House: 1st
Element: Fire
Symbol: Mars' Shield
Day of the Week: Tuesday
Number: 9

Jupiter

Glyph: ♃

Favorite of many, Jupiter promises fortune and wisdom, especially when it is in a favorable placement. This planet influences higher education, luck, abundance, spirituality, travels, adventures, philosophical views, and expansion. This giant planet can be a good measurement for personal and spiritual growth. It can also show you where you are extra lucky in life or how you can be more fortunate.

This planet provides people with expenditure and good fortune. Naturally, it rewards humans when they channel the same energy toward others. In other words, this planet likes it when folks mirror the same generosity.

If you have been going through an unlucky streak, you can try to be attuned to this planet's power and channel it by being generous or more helpful to others in need.

The lesser-known traits are laziness, indulgence, and having unrealistic expectations that are highly optimistic.

Some people think that having a good placement means they do not get any negative traits. That is not exactly true. Even if the planet is placed in a good house or sign, it can still have a hard aspect highlighting its less desirable qualities.

Speaking of placements, Jupiter rules Sagittarius and Pisces and the 9th house. It is exalted in Cancer, domicile in Sagittarius and Pisces, detriment in Gemini, and falls in Capricorn.

The number three and this planet go hand-in-hand because they are both big on expenditure. However, number three, natives can maximize the good and the bad in their lives. They also like building or creating, which aligns with Jupiter's energy. They are natural helpers, so they are often found helping others, giving advice, or teaching. This planet is all about approaching life's problems with the outlook of a higher self, and that is exactly what these natives do.

Keywords:

- Higher mind
- Luck
- Wealth
- Philosophy
- Higher education
- Generosity
- Wisdom

Signs: Sagittarius and Pisces

House: 9th

Element: Fire

Symbol: A cross with the character Z for Zeus

Day of the Week: Thursday

Number: 3

Saturn

Glyph: ♄

Known as a great teacher, Saturn is often feared because of its ample power. This planet is responsible for your life lessons. It will relentlessly challenge you until you fix a certain issue holding you back from growth.

Saturn rules commitments, weaknesses, growth, responsibilities, control, restrictions, self-work, boundaries, and fears. It governs Capricorn and is a sub-ruler of Aquarius, which naturally makes it the lord of the 10th and 11th houses. The planet also influences skin, joints, teeth, and bones. It is exalted in Libra, docile in Capricorn, detriment in Cancer and Leo, and falls in Aries.

Like Mars, whether it has harsh aspects or not, Saturn is considered a malefic planet. This planet brings restrictions, emphasizes limitations, and highlights weaknesses. It challenges you and conjures tests left and right to teach you. Some view this as bad luck, while others see it as a learning opportunity. However, when you are under the heat, it is difficult to appreciate the learning process, which is why Saturn is seen as malefic.

Now that we have covered the basics, it is time to acknowledge why people fear Saturn. This planet is infamous for one reason, "Saturn Return." This phenomenon happens when Saturn has completed one trip around the sun and returns to its placement in the birth chart. This trip takes around 30 years which means that you will experience it three times in your life. You can expect it in your late 20s, late 50s, and late 80s.

So, what happens during this period? Well, you can expect significant life changes and real challenges. The kind of challenges that make you feel like the universe is conspiring against you. In reality, though, Saturn is trying to get you in shape. It knows your potential and *who you can be in this life*, so it toughens you up. It helps you face your fears and gives you opportunities to act right by yourself.

During this time, you might find yourself with a lot of responsibilities. They could be anything from relationships, financial issues, emergencies, or even how you show up to yourself. Things like self-care and self-love could be a theme here.

How these responsibilities show up depends on who you are and where you set the limit. The thing is, Saturn does not like self-restrictions; it tries to push you until you shed your old self with all its illusionary restrictions.

Some people experience identity crises or feel like everything is falling apart. There is no denying that this phase is challenging but try to remind yourself that it is only temporary. Be kind to yourself, and maybe by the end of your first Saturn return journey, you'll find a better you waiting at the other end!

Emotional strength, self-discipline, and self-love are not easy characteristics to come by. They are not inherited, and more often than not, one needs to be put in one situation after the other so that these traits are built-in for good.

Saturn Return's effect lasts about two years. So, you will be feeling its energy, especially by the end. If you rise to the occasion and allow Saturn to help you grow, you'll find yourself renewed and more mature. You will be like a snake that has just shed its skin – fresh and shiny.

If things do not go according to plan, try to refrain from beating yourself up. Self-compassion here is key. This planet gives us more than one chance to rise above our self-imposed limitations. Like Jupiter, Saturn also likes growth. However, it gives us different opportunities, and you'll be getting them more than once so you can be the person you were always meant to be.

Saturn's energy heavily influences the number eight natives. Numerology says that these people contain a lot of inner wisdom and knowledge. They have the tools to embark on their spiritual journey, and they do not pay much attention to worldly ideas, nor are they interested in the materialistic. This kind of higher-self mentality makes them naturally attuned to Saturn's raw energy.

Keywords:

- Discipline
- Responsibility
- Task Master
- Growth
- Life Lessons
- Restrictions
- Practicality
- The Teacher

Signs: Capricorn & Aquarius

Houses: 10th & 11th

Element: Earth

Symbol: Chronus' Sickle

Day of the Week: Saturday

Number: 8

Uranus

Glyph: ⛢

Breaker of tradition, Uranus is the ruler of autonomy, independence, revolution, science, the occult, astrology, psychology, and inventions. This planet likes the unusual and causes sudden changes, often violent. They are not the kind of changes you see coming – or even *expect*. They may seem out of character or come out of nowhere. If you or someone in your life is experiencing something similar, this may be the planet's doing.

There is no telling if these sudden shifts are good or bad; this is entirely subjective. However, the planet aims to make you grow more into yourself by experiencing the unusual.

Because of its eccentric qualities, it is the natural ruler of Aquarius and lord of the 11th house. It is exalted in Scorpio, domicile in Aquarius, detriment in Leo, and fall in Taurus. It also governs the ankles, nervous system, and the body's electricity.

This planet's placement is vital. It tells you where you are at your most unusual or untraditional. You will need to check the sign and house it is staying in to understand more about your eccentricity.

Uranus loves freedom and independence, so try to refrain from holding yourself back or minimizing your autonomy. Whether you are rebellious or not, this planet's energy will get you to act out if you have been restricting yourself. So, you might as well be as free and authentic as your Uranus' placement is.

Number four, natives are all about innovation, originality, and rebelliousness. They also tend to be strong and humble. They love to feel secure and have stability in their lives, so you can see how these people are in harmony with Uranus' energy.

Keywords:
- Change
- Independence
- Awakening
- Creativity
- Rebelliousness

- Nonconformity
- Freedom
- Revolutionary
- Higher mind

Sign: Aquarius

House: 11th

Element: Air

Symbol: Letter H, after the discoverer Herschel

Number: 4

Neptune

Glyph: ♆

In astrology, Neptune is one of the more subtle planets. It is not that it is less powerful; it is that people do not notice its effects right away. This planet rules illusion, dreams, psychic abilities, subconscious, music, and art. It also influences spiritual enlightenment, universal love, and compassion.

Some of its negative traits are deceit, confusion, brain fog, hazy vision, addiction, and guilt. The traits that you get from Neptune depend on where it is placed and its aspects with other planets and luminary bodies.

This planet governs the pineal gland, kinesthetic functions, nerve fibers, and telepathic functions in the brain when it comes to anatomy.

It is the natural ruler of dreamy Pisces and the 12th house. It is exalted in Leo, domicile in Pisces, detriment in Virgo, and fall in Aquarius.

The planet's placement tells you where you are deceiving yourself or others. You might not be deceiving yourself on purpose, though. Neptune gives hazy memories sometimes, so you might not accurately recall things as they were, or your mind might be spewing lies about who you are.

Neptune governs people with 7 as their number since they are just as spiritual and enlightened. They are also just as imaginative and artistic as the planet. They could easily slip into their fantasies regarding their social circles. However, since they are naturally attuned to the planet, Neptune will remove any illusions when they are ready to see the truth.

Keywords:

- Subconscious
- Oneness
- Disillusionment
- Anxiety
- Addiction
- Dreams
- Enlightenment
- Strong intuition

Signs: Pisces

House: 12th

Element: Water

Symbol: The trident of Neptune

Number: 7

Pluto

Glyph: ♇

As you may already know, Pluto is one of the smallest and slowest planets, but these qualities do not mirror its effects, which are certainly drastic. This planet is all about destruction, the kind that can end rigid systems and countries. This is where the death part comes in. But Pluto is not that shallow. It also loves to build from the ground and create something from nothing.

Pluto is not always literal with death. For instance, it can kill an identity and create another in due time. This binary relationship of birth and rebirth is Pluto's rawest quality and one that is strongly felt.

It also governs isolation, dictatorships, viruses, phobias, masses, and obsessions. It also reveals deep secrets and rules anything that undergoes the replication process.

This planet rules Scorpio and the eighth house. Astrologists have not assigned where Pluto is exalted and where it is in fall. However, it is domicile in Scorpio and detrimental in Taurus. It also governs the reproductive system and pituitary gland. It can also cause moles, tumors, and birthmarks.

As you might have noticed, this planet is extremely slow. You might not undergo a Pluto return since it will take approximately 248 years to return to its place in your birth chart. This does not mean that you will not experience meaningful transformation in your life. Depending on the planet's aspects – especially when it is in transit – it will tell you everything you need to know about your Plutonian experience.

Now that you have familiarized yourself with Pluto's pace, you have probably guessed that it is a generational planet. In other words, almost every generation has the same Pluto sign, but the house is entirely different. You can use this to learn more about your generation or the one before you.

As previously mentioned, Pluto is all about death and rebirth. This cycle could not have been better represented other than by the number 0. That void and nothingness are frightening, but the planet promises that a lot can come out of nothing. Number 0 natives go through major transformations in their lives, which is exactly why they have such Plutonian energy.

Keywords:

- Transformation
- Death
- Rebirth
- Darkness
- Manipulation
- Abuse
- Taboos

Sign: Scorpio

House: 8th

Element: Water

Symbol: Letters PL symbolizing the planet's name

Number: 0

Chiron

Glyph: ⚷

Known as the "wounded healer," Chiron shares some painful truths and enlightening solutions. This minor planet tells us about our most extensive wounds in this life and how to tend to them. It shows you how deep your wound is and how you express or suppress it. You will learn how it manifests in your life and whether it is festering or not.

Depending on Chiron's placement, you can understand where you are overcompensating and whether or not you are neglecting your pain. Neglect here does not mean that you are intentionally ignoring your pain. Rather, it means that you could be in denial or unaware of the problem.

Another thing you might want to check is Chiron's aspects. What kind of aspects does it have with the other planets? Are these aspects harsh or harmonious? Aspects can tell you a lot about the nature of your sadness and how you feel about it emotionally, mentally, and spiritually.

Unlike other planets, Chiron does not rule anything per se. The only thing it truly wants is to help heal you. Think of this minor planet as a guide to ease your deep pain. It has a lot of wisdom to share with you, but you first need to find more about it yourself.

Uncovering your Chiron placement might be difficult to deal with since it tends to be triggering for people who are not aware of the problem. This is why the planet advises you to brace yourself and accept whatever your wounds are. Self-compassion and empathy are key here, and these are the first things you need to give yourself when exposing your wound to Chiron's healing energy.

Depending on the kind of aspects it has, Chiron might share the origins of your wound. You can also expect to have more than one major wound. This can be tough but remember that the planet will tell you how to self-heal.

True healing starts with patience and kindness with the self. It is okay if you are unsure how to begin the healing journey; no one knows at first. However, the more you learn from this planet and self-reflect, you'll find that your healing journey is unfolding right before your eyes.

Keywords:

- Wounded healer
- Introspection
- Acceptance
- Self-love
- Spiritual healing
- Emotional pain
- Inner child

Symbol: Key, a way to heal.

Chapter 3: The Zodiac Signs

In this chapter, you'll find an extensive description of each zodiac sign's energy. It is important to note that the following characteristics do not apply fully to every Aries or Libra person. An Aries sun sign might have some of these traits, but they will not embody every other trait because everyone's personality is unique. Given that everyone has a natal chart that is specific to them, a person's sun sign is not enough to describe a whole person. Unlike sun signs which are only one part of the story, the planets' placements and the kind of aspects they have with one another make up the full picture.

You may also want to pay attention to all signs, not just your sun sign. Every sign and its effects are included in your natal chart. To understand their energy and characteristics, familiarize yourself with them, and be able to analyze your birth chart.

Aries ♈

Season: March 21 - April 20

There is a lot to understand about the first sign of the zodiac through its placement. The sun lands on Aries at the beginning of each Spring. The earth starts to breathe again during this season, flowers bloom, and leaves grow. This newborn energy is mirrored in this sign.

The world is new to a child. Everything is yet to be explored and experienced. This is how Aries views life. They tend to enter new phases with enthusiasm and wide-open eyes. They do not mind juggling things because they have the energy for it. Their motivation is contagious. They give off radiant energy that remarkably energizes people around them. There is a deep-seated need to be kept busy with an Aries. They know that when their energy is not channeled, it can turn into frustration or aggressive behavior.

Their child-like energy can also turn into an immature attitude or mindset. Children are not expected to put other people's feelings first or think about them in the first place. They are still experiencing life from their point of view. This applies to Aries as well, and they tend to have a "me first" attitude. They can easily fall into a slippery, selfish attitude that isolates them. Aries tend to be impatient, so they act impulsively, which gets them into trouble. Aries people are advised to avoid setbacks by taking calculated risks.

Another interesting thing about the Aries placement is that it is opposite to Libra. Venus, the planet of beauty, rules Libra. Aries have a similar energy, so they tend to be physically attractive or have nice smiles.

To further comprehend this sign, you might want to familiarize yourself with the planet that rules it, Mars. This planet is full of rigorous wild energy. Aries are charged with this energy, and they tend to use it for Mars-related activities, such as sports, sex, work, and healthy competition. However, it goes beyond the fact that they are affected by its energy. Understand that Aries is associated with a seriously demanding planet, so it will make Aries channel this energy somewhere. Otherwise, they can become aggressive, bored, and frustrated.

Aries are very competitive.
https://pixabay.com/images/id-567950/

Aries is represented by the Ram. These animals are infamous for their fighting style, simply described as head-butting. This is how Aries instinctively fights or debates. They don't take time to contemplate, and their fiery attitude quickly turns a heated discussion into a full-blown fight.

Like rams, Aries are naturally stubborn. This is one of their lesser appreciated qualities. People will feel more appreciated around Aries when they feel like they are being listened to. Sometimes Aries unconsciously devalue people's words, which ends up with them feeling like they do not want to share personal information anymore.

Generally, people like their fiery attitude, but it is not always appreciated when they are argumentative. Aries are known for unnecessarily burning bridges. They do not hold grudges, but they do deal with accumulated resentments. The longer they harbor grudges, the more tiresome they will feel. Aries need to learn to let go. The more they mature, the more they realize that burning bridges is not always the ideal solution.

As previously mentioned, every sign has its modality. Aries is a cardinal. This means that this sign is an initiator in every aspect of life. They are natural leaders and often start things, projects, relationships, etc. Being a cardinal is one of their strongest assets. The only thing that needs work is completing what they have started - which should be easy, given their endless energy! The only thing standing in the way is boredom. Once it is fixed, Aries will finish projects left and right.

Keywords:
- Leader
- Competitive
- Present Oriented
- Independent
- Eager
- Brave
- Selfish
- Arrogant
- Childish
- Aggressive
- Domineering

Symbol: The Ram
Key Phrase: "I am"
Modality: Cardinal
Element: Fire
Planetary Ruler: Mars
Opposite Sign: Libra
House: 1st

Taurus ♉

Season: April 21 - May 20

The season of Taurus begins in the middle of spring. It is also the second sign in the zodiac. This placement alone gives enough information to understand what this sign is about. Taurus likes to be surrounded by beauty and comfortable company. Think of good music, tasty food, loyal friends, and family members.

Taurus has an interesting placement because it is opposite Scorpio. Generally, any two signs that are opposite one another share similar characteristics. Genitals rule Scorpios, so they crave good sex. Taurus is the same. Taurus is ruled by senses, so they go through life experiencing and enjoying it through their senses. Good sex life is a must for a Taurus. Without a good sex life, they might feel like something vital is missing from their life. Scorpio is possessive, as is Taurus.

Taurus might be a bit possessive over their loved ones. Of course, not every Taurus has that ownership mentality. However, depending on the level of maturity, they can be extremely possessive or do not understand that they do not own their partner.

This zodiac sign is known for its great emotional strength, patience, and loyalty. This comes from their symbol, the bull. This animal is patient and generally relaxed. It likes soaking in the Sun and doesn't like moving around much. Taurus has the same traits.

This is not to say that all Taurus are lazy. However, some would rather live life by relaxing and enjoying materialistic pleasures if given a choice. They are also exceptionally loyal, and they are admired for it. This sign is dependable and known for its support when needed. This acts as a double-edged sword because while Taurus enjoys that people depend on them, they also feel hurt when their support is not reciprocated.

They are known for both their patience and explosive anger. Unfortunately, for a Taurus, these two characteristics go hand-in-hand. However, thanks to their patience, they are not easy to trigger. Even when people try to push their buttons, they tend to hide their feelings or pretend that nothing affects them. But even a Taurus has limits. This is where the explosive anger comes in.

This zodiac sign is ruled by Venus, the planet of love, beauty, and finances. They are attractive people who are also attracted to beauty. They might be fond of all kinds of art and whatever is aesthetically beautiful. They might not feel at home if the place around them is untidy or unpretty to look at. Money is a concept that haunts their minds now and again. This is normal until it grows into an obsession with financial security.

This zodiac sign is an earth sign. They need stability and often provide it for other people. They are usually fixed in their behaviors and opinions, which rarely change. They are also fixated on their goals. They do not care about how long the process might be or what challenges they might face. Once they have set out to accomplish something, it is done.

Their love for stability often causes stress in relationships that change. They are not the most flexible when adapting and adjusting to changes in their lives. The more they grow, the more they can learn how to cultivate a healthier relationship with change.

Unlike Aries, Taurus likes to relax, settle, and enjoy life's pleasures, thanks to their fixed modality. Because they are more in tune with the natural rhythm of their lives, they are not one to initiate projects or friendships, and they do not feel the pressure to change anything about it.

Keywords:

- Stable
- Security seeker
- Loyal
- Stubborn
- Materialistic
- Patient
- Artistic
- Indulgent

- Dependable
- Explosive Anger
- Thorough

Symbol: Bull's Head
Key Phrase: "I have."
Modality: Fixed
Element: Earth
Planetary Ruler: Venus
Opposite Sign: Scorpio
House: 2nd

Gemini ♊

Season: May 21 - June 21

As the seasons change from spring to summer, the Gemini season begins. As previously mentioned, placements play a vital role in astrology. Gemini's duality and changeability mirrored the shift from one season to another. You get both sides: spring and summer. You also get versatility. This sign is known for its versatile moods and behaviors. Some would find these traits challenging to deal with, including Geminis themselves. If you are a Gemini yourself or have a friend who is, you might find yourself disliking the lack of stability that you get with this energy. Your mind can grow tired of the sign's unpredictability and its inability to anticipate what is coming next.

The planet of the mind and communication rules your sign. This influences you to seek knowledge. Generally, you like learning, and you are always chasing more knowledge. The thing is, almost everything interests you. Your curiosity is greedy, and you are always up for consuming educational content. You are a bit of a know-it-all, but your knowledge tends to be shallow. You usually scrape the surface unless it is something that you are generally interested in, then you go all the way.

Mercury also influences you to be somewhat of a social butterfly. You like talking to everybody and learning more about the people around you. You are either always texting, calling, or engaging in conversations with your friends or strangers. You do not mind talking about anything so long as it does not bore you. Sometimes when you are involved in a dull conversation, you try to take it in a more interesting direction.

Gemini is represented by the twins, or the Roman number two. There could not have been a better symbol for this sign as far as symbols go. The idea of twins is based on the sign's duality. If you are a sun sign Gemini, you are more than familiar with the eternal struggle between your mind and heart. You might feel that logically, you have figured it all out, but your emotions tend to sway the other way. This internal friction causes irritability, and this is most apparent when a Gemini exhibits unpredictable behavior due to mood swings.

You also vacillate and often find yourself changing opinions and certain beliefs. You might feel uneasy about this, so it is better to remind yourself that your mind is versatile. You see merit in everything. You are not known for your rigidity, nor do you resonate with this trait, and people appreciate that about you.

Gemini babies are generally sensitive and sympathetic. Not everyone might know this, but they feel for people, and words can hurt them, even though they tend to deny it. Even though Geminis are known for specific behaviors, other characteristics can go unnoticed, overshadowed by what the sign is notorious for.

It is not difficult for Gemini to change things up when life is stagnant. Their need for variety automatically adds spice to their life. This trait affects almost all aspects of their life. You like variety in friendships, the places you go to, reading, clothes, etc. They might not have a unified sense of style, but their overall style could be that they like different things and would not want to have it any other way.

Another quirky trait of Gemini is restlessness. It is not that they are generally lost and going back and forth with their thoughts; it is that they are physically restless as well. As a Gemini, it does not matter what kind of activity they are doing physically, as long as they are doing something. They might need to be tapping their fingers or feet, moving from side to side, humming, talking, or even fidgeting.

This trait also makes them great multi-taskers. They are not fond of tackling one thing at a time; tackling two or three is more their style. Imagine that a Gemini is reading a book. At the same time, they might be fidgeting with their hands or maybe listening to music. They might be dancing or listening to a podcast if they are showering. Even when watching a movie, they might be thinking about something else while keeping track of the events. It does not matter what they are doing, as long as they are doing another activity with it.

Gemini is one of the air signs with qualities like flexibility and social intelligence. Some people perceive this as hypocrisy. But the truth is, Geminis have high social awareness, so they know how to communicate with different groups, what kind of jokes to tell, and which stories to share.

However, one of the drawbacks is that this sign can be emotionally unstable. Geminis might feel uncomfortable with emotionally heavy issues. They do not like to go to the heart of the situation if it brings about unpleasant emotions. Air signs like to keep things moving, and stable situations, especially if they are heavy, go against this desire.

Geminis are part of the mutable club. They are slightly different from Cardinal and Fixed signs because they are more comfortable with change. If you are a Gemini yourself, you understand that change is a constant part of your journey and everyone else's. You are also agile in making necessary changes to adapt to a new lifestyle or situation that you have been put in.

Based on its duality, this sign rules symmetrical body parts and organs. Gemini influences your hands, collar bones, shoulders, and lungs. It also rules the nervous system because of its strong ties to the brain.

When it comes to a Gemini's love life, you can expect multiple partners, either one at a time or one after the other. This sign is not known for its emotional stability. As a Gemini yourself, you know how easy it is for you to grow bored of a relationship or a person. This explains your need for stimulation. Once a relationship is no longer fulfilling, you move on to the next one. You do not like being tied down, so one way you like to manifest your freedom is to come and go as you please.

As you grow older and allow yourself to emotionally mature, this trait will gradually dissipate from your life. You do not need to worry about being flighty in the meantime. However, do try to be sensitive and aware of other people's feelings.

Keywords:

- Social
- Communicative
- Versatile
- Inventive

- Restless
- Curious
- Literary
- Scatterbrained
- Ungrateful
- Low concentration
- Quick Witted

Symbol: Roman number 2
Key Phrase: "I think."
Modality: Mutable
Element: Air
Planetary Ruler: Mercury
Opposite Sign: Sagittarius
House: 3rd

Cancer ♋

Season: June 22 - July 22

Cancer - the momma sign. There are a lot of qualities to this sign, but it is mainly known for its nurturing - mainly due to its placement and ruling planet. Cancer governs the fourth house, which is affiliated with the caretaker's role and the family home. People born under this sign exhibit these themes in their lives. They naturally care for their loved ones, and their houses are usually comfortable and cozy.

This sign is also opposite to Capricorn, and with polarity comes similarity. A true Cancerian cares about money in the same way a Capricorn does. Cancers are not generally greedy, but they do worry about security a lot. Financial security is a concept that freely roams a Cancerian's mind, especially if it is left unaddressed. Many Cancers spend their lives trying to gain more money even when they have enough of it, just because they are chasing after financial security.

Cancer is ruled by the moon, considering how moody this sign is. The moon phases change frequently, and so does Cancer's mood. Astrologically speaking, each phase affects this sign in a certain way.

The moon rules emotions and intuition, and since it rules this sign, it provides great emotional depth and high intuition. Your sensitivity can be considered both a gift and a curse, depending on how you view it. On one hand, you are in tune with your emotions and those of others, and you feel emotions on a higher level. This gives you a deeper perspective on life. On the other hand, feeling things that deeply can emotionally drain you. Also, emotional pain affects you on another level. It feels like something is ripping your soul apart when you are hurting.

The moon gifts you with the gift of intuition which manifests in small things like entering a room and feeling its energy. If you listen to it, your gut will be telling you things throughout the day, and the more you listen to it, the stronger it will become.

Most Cancerians are empaths. This means that you most likely feel what is going on with your friend without them telling you. You might be able to feel your pet's emotions. You can also feel plants and trees when you connect with them.

As previously mentioned, Cancers are nurturing, so they will be the people who initiate a connection with you, and during this friendship, you can expect them to care for you. They are the kind of friends who will remind you to take your meds or encourage you to go to therapy. They also create projects that can help them with their income. These endeavors do not have to relate to Cancerian themes, like cooking or nurturing. However, if these projects coincide with things that a Cancer is affiliated with, they will feel right at home.

Derived from its name, this sign is represented by the crab. There are so many similarities between them that this sign could not have had a better symbol. Like the crab, Cancers like to stay at home rather than be around many people. However, people feel at home with them. This is why most Cancers are certified introverts.

They are also snappy like the crab. They are not the type to fly off the handle, but if their buttons are pushed long enough or hurt by someone they love, you'll see these claws coming at you. They are also vindictive and can hold a grudge. They spend time plotting their revenge and waiting for the right moment to attack you. Cancers are also known to be manipulative when they want to be.

If you have ever watched a crab, you'll know that it never walks directly to its target but moves sideways to get to where it wants to be. Cancers are precisely like that. When they want something or someone, they always scan the environment, measure how safe it is, and start approaching.

Ironically, they have a tough exterior, given their sensitive and warm hearts. The crab has a sturdy shell, and so does a Cancer. Most Cancers do not look approachable, but you start seeing a softer side once you get to know them. Most Cancerians appear this way because they are trying to shield themselves from the world. They know that they are sensitive and strong, but they always feel the need to be secure, so they take comfort in their tough exterior.

Cancerian sensitivity is not just attributed to the moon but is also influenced by water. Water signs are generally emotionally deep and feel things to the core. They also absorb people's feelings and take them up as if they were their own. With Cancers being a water sign, there are usually layers to them. Once you think you know them, you discover another layer that needs to be peeled.

As you may have noticed, Cancer season begins with Summer, which is why it is part of the Cardinal Club. Like, Aries, Cancers are initiators. They go after what they are seeking, and it is easy for them to embark on a new project or a journey. The kind of things that a Cancer will initiate will either have to do with human connections or money.

Keywords:
- Intuitive
- Nurturing
- Loving
- Helpful
- Sensitive
- Quippy
- Sharp-tongued
- Vindictive
- Absorbent
- Manipulative
- Guarded

Symbol: The Crab

Key Phrase: "I feel."

Modality: Cardinal
Element: Water
Planetary Ruler: Moon
Opposite Sign: Capricorn
House: 4th

Leo ♌

Season: July 21 - August 22

Leo, the star sign. This sign has gained a bit of a reputation over the years. Most people understand that Leos are just egotistical individuals who always want to be center stage and that this is all there is to them. This assumption has some truth, but it is still highly inaccurate. Let us break things down so that this sign is understood for what it truly is.

Leo is ruled by the sun, which is the center of our solar system. The sun in Astrology rules ego, individuality, and confidence, so it is only natural that Leos will unapologetically resonate with these qualities. It is in their nature to want to be the center of attention, but their energy also calls for it. They just have this energy about them that grabs people's attention, wanted or not.

They walk with confidence and see life as their stage. Everything is a performance for them. This adds spice to their lives, but it is also difficult for them to let go and be vulnerable. Their need to act their way through life is diminished by self-work and maturity. Some Leos show their vulnerability to the people closest to them or those they trust enough to show this softer side.

Being in the spotlight and wanting attention is not all that there is to a Leo sign. They are also generous and loyal to their people. Once you have become part of their circle, they will be loyal to you and generous with their love, energy, and time.

In terms of placement, Leos are the opposite of Aquarius. Aquarians are generally loners who appreciate their alone time. On the other hand, Leos prefer to be surrounded by like-minded people. They are usually the glue that holds the group together or the group's center. This is not to say that Leos always have all of the attention, but they tend to lead the conversation or talk the most in the group. Astrologers have noticed that

---

July Leos tend to have diluted Leo characteristics, while August Leos are more concentrated in Leo energy.

As previously mentioned, the Sun rules Leo. The sun gives energy to every living thing and is vital for everyone. Leos walk the earth with that same self-important attitude. They just feel important. There is nothing wrong with being aware of your self-worth and value. But things can go south quickly with a Leo.

If the ego expands or becomes unhealthy, Leos can be easily entitled and careless with people's feelings. They might not be aware of their effect on you or anyone else. They still can empathize, but they don't think of how people might feel when they talk or behave in a certain way. This can get ugly quickly, and it could turn into a complete disregard for everyone's feelings because they believe that they are the center of the universe.

Most Leos like careers or hobbies that have to do with the arts and being on stage, whether literally or metaphorically. They are also most likely to become the CEO of a company or start their own business. Leos are fairly creative, so if they are lucky, they can end up in a career where they perform on stage, sing, dance, or even become public speakers.

The lion represents Leos. The lion is the jungle king, loud, feared, and respected – not to mention the fact that it is royalty. Internally, Leos feel like they are royalty. They walk with pride and confidence. They are also brave and not afraid to voice their opinion. The strength of the lion also resonates with Leo's energy. Leos can endure tough situations. However, when something hurts their ego, they heal in silence and then return to the spotlight.

It is a no-brainer that Leos are a fire sign. Fire signs are energetic and active. These traits have a very particular way of manifesting in Leos. Unlike Aries and Sagittarius, Leos embody these fiery qualities in a group setting, relationships, and work. They add electricity to their group dynamic. They are usually fun to have around, and it is easy for them to uplift people's moods.

Their fire element can make them argumentative. They do not usually back down from a fight. However, once they are in an argument, they need to feel that they have won or had the last word. The longer this goes on, it can be frustrating to the person on the receiving end, so it is important to communicate with them about their behavior. They are more approachable when they have cooled down. They might not take criticism easily, but they will appreciate that you are trying to maintain a friendship or a relationship with them.

Leos are part of the *fixed modality club*. This is why they are dedicated and committed to anything they set their minds to. It is not easy to get a Leo to do something that they do not want to do, but once a Leo employee or a friend is passionate about what they are doing or has a goal set in mind, there is no way to stop them.

Being a fixed, creative sign dedicated to their craft, they are most likely to accomplish something astonishing and make great strides in their chosen path. Some Leos are artistic by nature, so their hobbies include music, painting, and writing. Other Leos use their creativity in their jobs, like stand-up comedians or creative managers, marketing, etc.

Keywords:

- Creative
- Generous
- Idealistic
- Confident
- Romantic
- Dignified
- Dramatic
- Pretentious
- Status conscious
- Childish
- Overbearing

Symbol: The Leo

Key Phrase: "I feel."

Modality: Cardinal

Element: Water

Planetary Ruler: Moon

Opposite Sign: Capricorn

House: 5th

Virgo ♍

Season: August 23 - September 22

We now move from the energetic Leo to the practical Virgo. This sign's placement is highly interesting. Virgo comes after a fiery and energetic sign that is prone to miss a detail, so Virgo offers patience and an eye for details. It is also opposite to Pisces, which is interesting because both signs have widely different ways of approaching life. However, both love helping people out, and the idea of being of service to others is something that they hold in high regard.

Virgo is ruled by Mercury, which symbolizes the mind and rules mental faculties. Mercury shrouds this sign with high analytical energy. They are extremely observant and hardly miss any details. Mercury's sharp intelligence and communicative nature mix well with Virgo's complexities. This mixture gives Virgo people the unique ability to point out inconsistencies, benefit their people, and affect positive change.

Sometimes, people perceive Virgos as pushy and naggy, but they are actually just trying to help out. Understand that this sign's nature is compelled to serve others. This sign's communication style might seem harsh at first, but the picture becomes a bit clearer when you understand their psyche.

Virgos will shamelessly point out things that are no longer serving you and habits hindering your progress. It is their way of showing that they care for you, and that is how they offer help. They might be the type of friends who check if you have finished your daily tasks or taken practical steps to reach your goals. They are the type of friends who remind you of doctor's appointments or take you to the doctor without asking. They might push you when you are slacking or procrastinating.

Mercury has blessed them with an acute mind that can design systems, stay focused, and prioritize rationality. This is why it is easy for them to get things done and help others complete their tasks. Their rationality makes them budget-conscious, so you'll find them creating budgets for friends or saving their money in multiple savings accounts.

Like Gemini, Virgo is also mutable. This results in the ability to adapt to different situations. They do not necessarily welcome change like air or fire signs, but they are flexible enough to survive whatever life throws at them. The only thing that might hold them back is their perfectionist tendencies. Virgos try to perfect everything they do, but with this comes a brain that is on high alert all the time, which can cause constant tension that could lead to anxiety.

The darker side of this is that they can be overly meticulous, making them feel like their skills and hard work are not enough. This will lead to disappointment and feelings of inadequacy, which is far from the truth. They also hold themselves to extremely high standards, which can exhaust them and leave them feeling burnt out. At the same time, they might not accept they have reached a point of exhaustion, so they try to make things work. At this point, they might find the quality of their work is flavorless, and they will be prone to blaming themselves instead of acknowledging that they are tired and deserve a break.

Virgos are represented by the virgin. The following story is recounted in Ancient Greek mythology. When Zeus sent Pandora's Box as a punishment for mankind, Astraea, the Goddess of innocence and purity, was curious about the contents of the mysterious box. Once she opened it, the box released various evils into the world. Saddened by the fate of humans, she took refuge in the heavens and became the constellation known as Virgo.

This myth gives us a deeper understanding of the Virgo sign. Virgos have high feminine energy, which makes sense since a Goddess represents them. They are also pure like Astraea, but their purity shows more in the kind of work they produce. They like their work to be flawless and perfect. They are also private and secretive, so they observe everything in silence while they may appear shy and quiet. They may appear reserved at first, but that is not their true nature.

Virgo is an earth sign. This tells you that they are fixed in their ways, so it is challenging to sway their beliefs or opinions. It also tells you that they are quite reliable, which makes sense, given their work ethic and love of service. They also like accomplishing goals, giving themselves tiny tasks to finish every day. The idea is that they like having something to do, so they might spend time cleaning everything and making sure that everything is spotless as part of their daily-chores routine.

They are also part of the mutable club. They tend to be easygoing if it does not concern their high standard. But once they have been asked to help, they will be implementing their unyielding methods. They will want to make you reach perfection, which might be unrealistic, but this is how Virgo completes their tasks. They hold very high standards for themselves and everyone else, and while this work ethic could be beneficial, it is also draining at times.

Keywords:

- Practical
- Kind
- Sensible
- Organized
- Modest
- Humane
- Headstrong
- Self-centered
- Critical
- Overthinking
- Uptight

Symbol: The Virgin

Key Phrase: "I analyze."

Modality: Mutable

Element: Earth

Planetary Ruler: Mercury

Opposite Sign: Pisces

House: 6th

Libra ♎

Season: September 23 - October 22

Libra has an interesting placement. It is the seventh sign of the zodiac and is opposite Aries and right before Scorpio. These placements have shaped this sign's characteristics. Aries are more self-centered and can often be unconsciously selfish. Libras are the opposite being more socially conscious, and they tend to think of others before themselves.

While this is a beautiful trait to have, sometimes, Libras hurt themselves. They naturally gravitate toward people, and they want to please people because they love harmony. On the brighter side, though, this sign is known for its social intelligence and awareness. They usually know the right thing to say, and they know how they behave around certain people. Their social intelligence makes them know how to take care of you and whether or not it is time to be a good listener or try to help.

Another interesting fact about this sign's placement is that it is right before Scorpio, making them share a few similarities with the sign. Like Scorpios, Libras can be relatively sharp-tongued, and so they might hurt someone by only using their words.

It is not often that you'll witness a visibly angry Libra. This sign likes balance and harmony, but when someone has tipped their scales and a Libra is unhappy, they will start speaking.

Naturally, Libras avoid fights, conflicts, and confrontations at all costs. However, the day they start a conflict is a day that you know they cannot suppress it anymore. This kind of suppression leads to an eruption of hurtful words because Libras will usually speak the truth. The truth, in this case, might be ugly, and while it is something that you might not want to hear, it is something that a Libra could not hold in any longer.

Like Taurus, this sign is ruled by Venus, the planet of feminine energy, love, beauty, and relationships. This makes Libra quite the artist because they have a natural appreciation for anything that emanates beauty.

Influenced by the planet, they care a lot about relationships, whether they are romantic or intimate friendships. They might seem aloof to you at first, but they often observe and analyze their environment. Their aloofness does not mean they are not seeking a person they can share their lives with. Libras appreciate companionship. To them, everything goes in two, like the scales. Companionship brings harmony and balance to their lives, and so it is something that they unconsciously seek.

Libras are ruled by scales. In other words, balance is vital for them. This manifests in every area of Libra's life. They require emotional balance and physical balance. They need balance in conversations, so they like a good give-and-take. They do not like it when dialogue turns into a monologue, and they appreciate it when people are mindful of this. Interruptions could be considered a pet peeve for Libra.

Libra is an air sign, so no wonder they like to observe, analyze, and communicate. They might stay in their head for a while, but they have a lot to share once they are present. Usually, when they avoid a conflict, they think about what to say or how to act the next time they see the person who wronged them. Libras can be hurtful with their angry words, so more evolved Libras like to take their time before speaking.

Their communication skills are also enhanced by their air quality. As you know by now, air signs love socializing and communicating with another person. This is why this sign appreciates bouncing ideas off other people. They can make up their minds by themselves, but they prefer to have someone with them during this process.

This sign is also part of the cardinal club, and they, too, are initiators. However, Libras are likely to initiate things that go hand-in-hand with their interests. This means that Libras are more likely to initiate a conversation with a stranger or new colleagues. They come up with suggestions about a fancy date night or request quality time with you.

Keywords:
- Aesthete
- Diplomatic
- Charming
- Peace-loving
- Strategic
- Sophisticated Taste
- Superficial
- Indecisive
- Indifferent
- Easily distracted
- Conflict avoidance

Symbol: The Scales
Key Phrase: "I balance."
Modality: Cardinal
Element: Air
Planetary Ruler: Venus
Opposite Sign: Aries
House: 7th

Scorpio ♏

Season: October 23 - November 21

As mentioned before, Scorpio is the opposite of Taurus. This is why they have similar traits. Taurus enjoys life through the five senses, and Scorpios are the same, in a way. As the genitals rule this sign, sex plays an important role in their lives. It is not just the act itself, but more of what it means and its effect on them. It exists in their lives with great intensity, and it could be the cause of great pleasure or great guilt and shame. Either way, Scorpios chase that feeling and reach their gratification through sex.

Scorpios are also similar to Taurus when it comes to an ownership mentality. They are naturally controlling as a result of trust issues. Most people born under this zodiac sign have developed trust issues during childhood. They most likely idealized a parent or parents who betrayed their trust. As a result, a Scorpio is deeply hurt by this betrayal, and they do not put themselves in vulnerable positions easily. Hence, the control and ownership mentality.

If you are involved with a Scorpio, you'll notice how they chase you, and once they have you, they think they own you. This is brought on by their Plutonian intensity and lack of trust in people.

Pluto rules this zodiac sign. This planet's energy is immersed in themes such as transformation, death, rebirth, the occult, mysticism, and anything taboo in nature. This planet affects Scorpios to the core. They naturally carry that transformative energy within them, for better or worse. That does not mean that they are easily swayed or change their opinions easily. However, they have a unique ability to change someone's life.

When Scorpios' intentions are good, they can be incredibly loyal to you. Their strong commitment and determination bring this about. Scorpios have a gift for seeing the potential in everything, so a Scorpio will see it for you even if you do not see your potential. They will want to share their gift with you, and they will transform your life for the better. Your life will change into something you had no idea it could be.

Scorpios are naturally brave. They are not afraid to speak their mind, and they don't shy away from standing up to themselves or their loved ones. The confidence and charisma they have makes it possible for them to speak freely without fearing the consequences.

Scorpios tend to live their lives from one end of the spectrum or the other, but never in the middle. In other words, they are extreme beings. Everything they do, and even how they think, is always taken to the extreme. They do not fathom life's murky gray, where things are not necessarily crystal white or pitch black. Again, this is caused by Pluto's intensity on this sign.

Pluto is affiliated with the hidden and anything dark or mysterious. This is reflected in Scorpios' innate secrecy. They are naturally secretive, although not intentionally secretive all the time. If you are friends or involved in any way with a Scorpio, you might notice that they probably know more about you than you know about them. Some things they just keep to themselves. This can be traced back to their lack of trust or their knack for revenge.

This zodiac's symbol is widely misunderstood. People think that a scorpion represents it, but the scorpion's tail represents this sign. Why the tail? Because it is painful, violent, and at times, deadly.

If you have ever observed a scorpion kill its prey, you must have noticed how sneaky and quiet it was; how it latched its stinger onto the prey, only letting go once the stinger had sunk in. This is how a Scorpio bites in real life. They do not let go of things that have hurt them, and they are not the forgetful type either. Pain does not sit easily within them, so they plan for their next sting.

Scorpios are a water sign. This fact alone should speak volumes about their intuition, emotional depth, and intensity. Water signs feel things to the core, and Scorpios are no different. Their intuition is strong, even if they are unaware of it. They can tell if someone is being manipulative or inauthentic just by looking into their eyes.

This zodiac sign is also part of the fixed signs club. This tells you that they are naturally committed to anything they believe in. They are hard workers and can be serious when necessary. They might be a bit stubborn, and you cannot change their opinions easily, but it is not impossible to do so.

Keywords:
- Resourceful
- Motivated
- Aware
- Passionate

- Probing
- Secretive
- Intense
- Revengeful
- Violent
- Controlling
- Suspicious

Symbol: Scorpion's tail
Key Phrase: "I desire."
Modality: Fixed
Element: Water
Planetary Rulers: Pluto and Mars
Opposite Sign: Taurus
House: 8th

Sagittarius ♐

Season: November 22 – December 21

Sagittarius is the ninth zodiac sign and is opposite Gemini. This placement means they share similar qualities, like their extroverted energy and high social skills. Sagittarians love communicating with everybody. They appreciate talking with you and learning from you.

Sagittarians are truth-seekers, so it is a journey to get to the real you when they are speaking to you. They are not interested in who you portray yourself as or the surface levels of who you are.

Like Geminis, they, too, love to learn. They have a hunger for knowledge and like to experience it in abundance. In other words, they are not satisfied when they learn through one method. They would rather get their knowledge from different sources and in various ways.

They learn from people by observing them. If they are sitting with you, they might learn about your psyche and behavior as a human being and register this knowledge with previous experience. So, it is not so much any advice that you might share; it is more about how you behave, act, and react.

Not only are they truth-seekers, but they are also truth-speakers. For better or worse, Sagittarians are blunt. You know where you stand in their lives because they will tell you the truth loud and clear. The way they express their honesty may hurt, so they might want to work on being sensitive to others. But on a more positive note, you'll never have to wonder whether they are telling the truth or not.

This does not mean that they never lie, but Sagittarians do not feel the need to hide their truth in the moments that count. In other words, what you see is what you get.

This zodiac sign is ruled by Jupiter, the planet of good fortune. Sagittarians carry this natural luck with them, even when they are going through a rough patch. If they are experiencing loss, something good might come out of it. Sometimes their good luck is found in their ability to notice the positives in everything, even in bad situations.

Jupiter is about adventure and expansion, and Sagittarius is no different. They are especially adventurous people. They appreciate any new life experience that will enrich their lives.

They also have a little philosopher who resides within them. They often wonder about life's deeper questions, and they are not afraid to look deeper within their minds or to an outside source to find the answers to their questions.

This also makes them spiritual people. Spirituality and religion are different, and they can feel this difference in their hearts. They might be in touch with the hidden energies that roam the universe and feel their effects in their day-to-day lives.

They are also fairly optimistic people and have an extraordinary ability to spread their cheer wherever they go. Of course, this only happens when they are in a good mood, but Sagittarians are not known to be a grumpy sign.

The archer represents this sign. The archer is free, independent, and accurately fixates on what he wants to reach. This zodiac sign embodies the same qualities. Their freedom is valuable to them, and they would not easily compromise it.

They are independent thinkers and live their lives in the same way. Sagittarians do not like to be tied down to situations or people, so they would rather live independently without anyone's influence on their freedom.

Once they have a target and their goal is clear, they aim for it without hesitation. They are determined to reach what they seek without being burdened by fear or responsibility like the archer.

They might have a few commitment issues, but they can work on them as soon as they understand what it means to be independent, even in a relationship. They might need to learn more about the art of compromise, but nothing is really out of reach once they have their eyes fixated on it.

This zodiac sign is a fire sign, so you can already understand the reason behind their passionate personality. They have a fire that ignites their desires, energy, and hunger for knowledge consumption. They are also fairly active individuals and act on proactive goals to reach their destination.

They are also part of the mutable club. They might be a bit restless now and then and go through a scatter-brained phase, but once they snap from it, they are back to their focused self again. Like the rest of the mutables, they have a natural ability to add their creativity to improve anything they set their eyes on.

Keywords:

- Philosophical
- Straightforward
- Athletic
- Optimistic
- Strategic
- Just
- Blunt
- Pushy
- Chatty
- Impatient
- Exaggeration

Symbol: Archer's arrow

Key Phrase: "I understand."

Modality: Mutable

Element: Fire

Planetary Ruler: Jupiter

Capricorn ♑

Season: December 22 – January 21

When it comes to placement, this zodiac sign is the opposite of Cancer. Cancers are serious about having a home for themselves. They like the idea of family, and they don't take it lightly. Capricorns are very similar in this respect.

Capricorns tend to have a traditional mindset when it comes to family life. They want a serious life partner who is as dedicated as they are, and they want to build a home and make a family with them.

Normally, they will not rush to find someone suitable. However, they will always watch for a potential life partner. They are most likely to observe everybody in the background, so they know who to take seriously and who to cast aside.

Even though Capricorns have had their fair share of hardships, this does not mean that they do not know how to unwind and have fun. They take on similar characteristics of a Cancer and emulate them. They, too, can be funny and are sometimes silly. When they are in the mood to make people laugh, their sense of humor tends to be sarcastic.

Saturn rules this sign, and it emulates a lot of the planet's qualities. Like the planet, Capricorns have a mindset that revolves around ambition, goals, and structure. They are usually clear about what they want to do in life and have enough stamina to reach it.

Dedication and commitment are almost second nature to Capricorns, and they are aware of these concepts early on in life.

Influenced by Saturn, most Capricorns have experienced a difficult childhood. They might have had to grow up too soon or understand the weight of responsibility early on. Saturn's mission is to mold you into the best version of yourself, even if the process is ugly. This kind of energy influences them, so they are used to struggling to reach their destination. They are more used to things going wrong for them, so they do not naturally have high expectations.

The goat is the symbol for this sign. This is reflected in how a Capricorn deals with life. They know they have a high mountain to climb, and they understand that the road may not always be smooth. But this does not discourage them. They climb the mountain and walk over sharp rocks to reach the peak. The process may be slow, but they know they will get there in due time.

A Capricorn's progress might be slow. It might take them years to reach their goals. However, they never lose sight of their plans, and they wake up every day and complete tasks that serve their purpose. It is not difficult for them to succeed or reach high places in society because they have the right mentality and enough stamina to follow through.

This sign is an earth sign. This gives them an edge when it comes to their organizational skills and time management. This element also reflects Capricorn's desire for public image. This sign cares a lot about how it is viewed in the public eye. It cares about social status and always wants to maintain its reputation. They care about their reputation and the reputation of anyone closely associated with them. To a Capricorn, their family and children also reflect their image to the public. So, they take matters like this to heart, and they are usually serious about it.

Capricorn is also part of the cardinal club. They dedicate this energy to adding and creating projects and plans that serve their drive and ambition. Unlike other cardinals, though, Capricorn commits strongly to their plans, so once plans are set in motion, there is no stopping a Capricorn.

Keywords:
- Hardworking
- Responsible
- Serious
- Professional
- Economical
- Cautious
- Egotistic
- Brooding
- Fatalistic
- Domineering
- Unforgiving

Symbol: Goats horn and tail
Key Phrase: "I use."
Modality: Cardinal
Element: Earth
Planetary Ruler: Saturn
Opposite Sign: Cancer
House: 10th

Aquarius ♒

Season: January 22 – February 21

As mentioned before, the opposition plays a detrimental role in Astrology. Remember that opposites attract because they have similar and different characteristics. Aquarius' placement is opposite to Leo's. Being strong humanitarians, they are loyal to their people. They care about the people in their lives, even when emotionally detached.

Emotional detachment is an Aquarius characteristic. Usually, with Leos, their emotions are dramatized on the surface. Aquarius is the complete opposite of that. It is something that they struggle with from time to time because it can reach a point where they doubt that they have any emotions.

On the contrary, Aquarius' *do have feelings*, but they do not exist on the surface, and they are skillful in hiding their feelings even from other Aquarius people.

People might find this trait difficult, but Aquarius' love, care, and loyalty smooth their emotional unavailability and detachment.

Like Leos, an Aquarius loves having friends. They care a lot about humans and humanitarian themes, so it is safe to say that they love being surrounded by people. They are sociable and love observing people react and interact. They gather information on their surroundings for educational purposes most of the time. They learn a lot about the human psyche from their interactions or from their observations.

Because of their social skills, they are very skilled at networking and usually have contacts from all walks of life. They make great members of any team involved in and enjoy different group activities.

Uranus rules this sign and has quite an influence on it. Aquarius is proudly unconventional. They will not succumb to societal rules on a grand scale, and the same could be said in their personal lives. They do not follow house rules or go with the flow in their peer groups.

They might have grown up feeling different from others. They might have felt alienated and struggled with relating to their surroundings. This took a toll on them during their childhood years, but they embraced that raw Uranus energy within them as they grew up.

You will find that Aquarius people express their originality in their clothing, art style, music, house decor, or anything seen publicly. They subconsciously make it a point to say, "I am different, I am original," and it shows.

They could be seen as rebellious, but the truth is that they are just individualistic, free people. They will not follow through with anything that compromises their freedom or stifles their originality.

Uranus gives them that coldness or detachment attitude. So, in a close relationship with an Aquarius, give them their space and distance. They will eventually open up to you when they are not being rushed. Understand that they do love you, but they cannot stand when anyone or anything affects their freedom.

The water-bearer is the symbol for this sign. Humans cannot live without water. It is an absolute necessity. The water here represents knowledge and invention. Technology and inventions would not have existed without basic knowledge. This is why these themes are associated with this sign.

They are inventive and avid knowledge seekers. They are here to bring new ideas to the forefront, no matter how unconventional or bizarre they may seem at first. Their mind is futuristic, and they often wonder about unconventional concepts that could be used for humanity.

Aquarius is an air sign, so they are talented in communication. However, they do know how to keep their distance when necessary. This sign is not comfortable with commitments because of its natural detachment. They might not be the most comfortable sign of emotional vulnerability, and they cannot grasp its importance.

Like other fixed signs, Aquarius is stubborn at times. But its fixed modality gives it the determination to follow through with its goals. Unlike other fixed signs, they are more open-minded to different opinions and ideas, but they will most likely listen to themselves at the end of the day.

Keywords:

- Progressive
- Intellectual
- Tolerant
- Scientific
- Altruistic
- Independent
- Rebellious
- Shy
- Cold
- Unpredictable
- Impersonal

Symbol: Water-bearer
Key Phrase: "I know."
Modality: Fixed
Element: Air
Planetary Ruler: Uranus
Opposite Sign: Leo
House: 11th

Pisces ♓

Season: February 22 – March 21

The final sign of the zodiac is Pisces. This sign's placement is interesting because it is often compared to Aries. Aries is the first sign, so it is almost like the baby of the zodiac, and you can view Pisces the same way.

Pisces are wise and have this "old soul" energy that resides within them. They are the last sign, which makes them in tune with the universe's energies.

They are naturally empathetic and understanding. People might mistake these traits for passivity, but it is quite the opposite. Pisces understands how humans and the world work. They do not feel the pressure to prove who they are or show off their capabilities to others because they understand that everything is finite.

They are also opposite of Virgo, so they also like to be of service to others. They are available to help others, whether emotionally or in any other area of life. They have ample generosity within them to give to others constantly.

Because of their high empathy and willingness to help, they will often self-isolate. People sometimes take this personally, but Pisces will need to sit in their corner and recharge. They are constantly connected to everyone's energy to the extent that they need to rest and return.

Neptune rules this sign. This speaks volumes about their spiritual and psychic abilities. They are effortlessly in tune with the universe, so they are naturally spiritual even if they are not aware of this yet.

Their imagination knows no limits. Fueled by Neptune, they can be dreamy and travel through worlds in their minds. They are not too attached to this realm because their minds are subconsciously in tune with different realms simultaneously. They are most likely to experience other realms with different dimensions in their sleep.

Their Neptunian energy is heightened when they partake in any spiritual activity, whether through meditation or by being in service to others. Their ruling planet also gives them a unique understanding of sex. For Pisces, sex is a spiritual act, and the more comfortable they are with their sexuality, the more open they become. Once they reach this state of inner peace with their sexuality, their energy and appearance change, they feel like they are more open to others, and their presence is comforting and welcoming.

Neptune also gives them an ample appreciation for art, especially music. Pisces feels music on an energetic level. They are the type to feel the lyrics or feel the music to their core. Most of them are naturally talented when it comes to instruments. Others just have a rich appreciation for music in general.

This planet also makes a Pisces somewhat of an escapist. Sometimes life gets too hard for them, and they would rather escape into another world, whether it is through a book or a movie. Others escape by using certain substances that would not be categorized as especially healthy. As long as Pisces copes with a healthy amount of escapism, they should not be facing any problems.

This sign is symbolized by two fish going in opposite directions. One fish is connected to reality, and the other to the spiritual realm. One fish wants to accomplish earth-related goals, like a job, career path, money, and status. The other fish wants to take care of energetic levels and help others with their energy and spirituality.

This can cause a struggle for Pisces as they go back and forth between the demands of both realms. This is also why they have difficulty being practical with realistic goals.

They are also spiritual healers, so they are highly sensitive and sympathetic. They will help you heal in different areas in life, but you too have to show that you care about them.

Their water element also brings on their sensitivity. Like its other water sisters, they feel emotions on a deeper level. They can get lost in their emotions because of their Neptunian energy. They are connected to their emotions but not blinded by them, but they can easily get lost.

They are also a mutable sign, so they are fairly easygoing, and they have a lot of creativity to share with others. Usually, when they are handed a task, they add their creative touch to that task and make it much better than when it was delivered to them.

Keywords:
- Dreamy
- Introspective
- Musical
- Scientific
- Altruistic
- Independent
- Pessimistic
- Melancholic
- Indolent
- Timid

Symbol: Two fish joined together
Key Phrase: "I believe."
Modality: Mutable
Element: Water

Planetary Ruler: Neptune

Opposite Sign: Virgo

House: 12th

Chapter 4: The Twelve Houses

The natal chart is divided into twelve sections called houses. In astrology, houses are ruled by certain planets and signs. The rulership is based on shared themes between the houses, signs, and planets. For instance, the moon rules Cancer because it is related to maternal instincts, mothering, nurturing, childhood house, and general feminine energy. These themes coincide with the fourth house and are, therefore, ruled by the moon and Cancer.

Note that this is considered the perfect placement if you have the moon or Cancer in the fourth house. This luminary body or sign is in harmony with its placement. Of course, this does not always mean that you had the perfect nurturing and the best childhood house, but depending on the planet's aspects, it is not a disadvantage.

The First House: The House of the Self

The ascendant takes place on the cusp of the first house. Your ascendant represents your outside persona in astrology, or rather how people perceive you. Generally, people do not get to see the real you once they meet you. But they do meet your ascendant. Let us say that your sun sign is in Libra and that your ascendant is in Capricorn to better understand this. This means that people view you as a Capricorn, and you act like one, but when they get to know you more, they meet your sun sign.

This is not to say that this is a fake side of you; it is very real. Think of it as the first layer of your personality. Your ascendant also plays a vital role in growing up, especially during childhood. That is to say that when you were a child, you were behaving per the ascendant sign, not the sun sign.

The ascendant also informs you how you'll act and present yourself during new phases in life. Every time you are in a new place, with new people, or have entered a new chapter, you behave like your ascendant sign. So, if you want to gain some insights into your mannerisms, you might want to check out your ascendant sign, which will be located on the cusp of the first house.

You also look like your ascendant. If your ascendant is Libra, then your body is well proportioned, and either your face or body is attractive. Astrologers have reached this conclusion based on the following factors: the ascendant's rulership, the ascendant's characteristics, and the first house's rulership. In this case, Libra is the ascendant, so Venus rules Libra, which implies physical beauty. Libra likes balance, hence the well-proportioned body. Aries rules the head, which suggests a beautiful face. You can apply the same logic to your ascendant sign. Think of it as an astrological mirror that you can look into and see your reflection.

The first house and the ascendant heavily shape your identity and ego. Your identity is your ascendant sign and the planets in the first house. Not everyone has planets in their first house. This does not necessarily signify anything, but you might want to read up on your ascendant sign if this is your case. However, if you have planets there, you might want to understand how they influence you and how they impact your ego.

Note that the planet that rules your AC sign is the planet that has rulership over your chart. Now, what does this mean? Chart rulership means that the planet that governs your AC sign is the planet that has the strongest effect on you. So, when this planet is in retrograde, transiting, or in progression, you will be affected by it the most. It is as if you are specifically sensitive to this planet's movement.

If you have Aries as your AC, then Mars has rulership over your chart. So, when Mars is transiting, and an aspect with another planet afflicts it, you'll feel this aspect heavily.

Keyword: Identity

Planet Ruler: Mars

Sign: Aries

The Second House: The House of Substance

The second house rules personal security. This includes financial, physical, and emotional security. Taurus, an earth sign, rules this section to better understand this. This means that this area of your chart represents your money and other materialistic items that you own. It also reflects your relationship with materialism and how you view your money.

For example, let us say that Aries is in your second house. This tells you that you are direct with how you get your money, and you have a lot of energy and creativity with how to obtain the amount of money you need. It also suggests that you are an entrepreneur or receive your income through independent projects. You also might be impatient and need to reap the seeds you have sowed immediately.

You can also get some insight into what you desire and how you wish to obtain it. Your desires might be a mystery to you at the moment, but by looking at this section, you can understand what you deeply need and want to have in your life. Based on this, you can understand what you attract in your life and how you attract it.

The second house is also linked with self-worth and value. How you perceive yourself and what you think about yourself are influenced by this house, its sign, and the planets in it. People with Neptune in the second house, for instance, may have illusions regarding their worth. It is either exaggerated or seen as way less than it is. Some people have false beliefs about themselves because of Neptune's influence.

To get a better insight, check your second house sign and see if there are any planets there. After you have done so, study the sign in this area of your natal chart and draw comparisons between it and how you view and behave around your possessions and self-worth. The same logic applies to the planets if there are any there. The planets will influence you to behave in a certain way, and you might exhibit some traits of said planet.

Keyword: Values

Planet Ruler: Venus

Sign: Taurus

The Third House: The House of Communication

Mercury and Gemini rule the third house, so the third house has to do with mental faculties. To understand this section better, you might want to look at its placement in the natal chart. The third house is opposite the ninth house. You know that opposition in astrology is not chance but always serves a purpose. The third house rules the cognitive part of the brain, while the ninth rules abstract concepts the mind generates. In other words, this area of the birth chart rules analytical thinking, communication, writing, logic, compartmentalization, and other left-brain functions.

If you are curious about your thinking process, how you come up with your thoughts, and how you communicate with others or yourself, you might want to check your third house sign to see if there are any planets there. To gain more insight into this part of your brain, you might want to check the aspects between planets in the third house and Mercury.

You can also learn about your attitude towards knowledge and learning. For instance, Scorpios in the third house might use knowledge to their advantage or be secretive with what they know. Scorpios will chase knowledge as long as it sparks their curiosity. They also tend to chase whatever is not on the surface. On the other hand, Leos may be generous with their knowledge once you are part of their circle.

The third house also rules relationships with siblings, cousins, aunts, uncles, and neighbors. The kind of placements in the third house can either resemble certain traits that your siblings have or characteristics that you project onto them.

This area of your birth chart also shapes your early school experience. You learned from your classmates and friends just as you did from your teachers during your school years. Additionally, astrologists say that several planets in the third house suggest that the person frequently changed environments while growing up.

Keyword: Awareness
Planet Ruler: Gemini
Sign: Mercury

The Fourth House: The House of Roots

The Imum Coeli, also known as IC, takes place on the cusp of the fourth house. Imum Coeli is the "bottom of the sky," referring to our roots. Themes like childhood, parents, home, family life, and internal life occur in the fourth house.

Your fourth house sign is a tell-tale sign of your childhood and what kind of child you were. Did you receive love? Did you grow up in a house that provided love and warmth? Or did you grow up in a cold and lonely environment? These are the kinds of questions you can ask yourself as you check this section of your birth chart.

The moon and Cancer rule the fourth house, so it is no surprise that the fourth house represents the mother and family life. If a cloud hovers over your relationship with your mother or your immediate family, you can seek this kind of knowledge from your fourth house sign.

You must pay attention to the planets that take place in this section. For instance, if you have Neptune in the fourth house, your parents might have had a deluded view of who you are as a person. They might have seen you as an extension of themselves or put you on a pedestal instead of treating you as a child.

If you have planets in the fourth house, it is best to study them and understand how they affected your childhood. Some people have their moon in the fourth house. This does not always mean that they had an affectionate mother. It could mean that they had to take the caretaker role early on in life, and no one nurtured them during their childhood years.

Astrologists say that the fourth house sometimes refers to the father, not just the mother. This is why it is best to view the fourth house as a section that portrays early family life, not necessarily just the relationship with the mother.

The fourth house is also connected with our soul. This means that planets in the fourth house and your fourth house sign will also describe you. For example, a person who has Capricorn as their fourth house sign could have grown up in a cold environment. It also means that, deep down, they are a hard-working person, and it is hard for them to open up about their emotions.

Keyword: Roots
Planet Ruler: The Moon
Sign: Cancer

The Fifth House: The House of Pleasure

The fifth house is ruled by the sun and Leo. Naturally, this house has to do with creative outlets, pleasure, and children. The fourth house reveals part of your identity deep down within you that you might have missed. But the fifth house is the exact opposite of that. This is the part of your identity that you most identify with or gives you the utmost pleasure.

Given that this part is ruled by the sun, which is ego, and Leo, who loves being in the spotlight, this is only natural. Various factors in the birth chart make up your unique personality. The fifth house represents a part of your identity that makes you shine and makes you unique.

Your fifth house sign reveals where your creativity and unique persona peak. Engaging in harmonious activities with your fifth house sign can make you feel like you are on top of the world. It gives you pleasure and brings you happiness. This is why this section rules your pleasure in life.

This section in your natal chart also rules children. You might find this odd at first, but the sun gives life to everything, and so it is the ruler of the fifth house. Naturally, this part rules children too.

This does not always mean that you will have children during your lifetime. However, it could show the role of children in your life. Individuals with Jupiter in the fifth house have a very high chance of having children of their own. Others have Uranus in their fifth house, which could mean that they might adopt or be a mother or father figure to the children in their lives.

You can also learn more about your talents through this area in your birth chart. People with Scorpio in their fifth house might delight in doing some detective work as a hobby. They might enjoy practicing, making, or reading more about the occult. Given the sexual nature of Scorpios, they also might enjoy a rich sex life.

Engaging in any harmonious creative outlet with your fifth house sign is important. This will give you a sense of true joy, where you are truly in your element. For instance, signs in the fifth house, like Taurus, might be great chefs and enjoy making food for others. Cancers might like designing homes, creating a cozy ambiance, or being wedding decorators. Pisces might get lost in music and photography, and they might spend most of their time singing, making music, or taking pictures.

Find out which sign resides in your fifth house and check if there are any planets there. To get more insight into this, you might want to check what kind of aspects these planets have with your sun. You can understand more about how you like to exert creative effort and learn more about your ego and identity through this.

Keyword: Creativity

Planet Ruler: The Sun

Sign: Leo

The Sixth House: The House of Service

Mercury and Virgo rule the sixth house. Naturally, this house is associated with service and duty. This section shows you how you could be of service to others. This does not always mean service throughout your career; it could just be how you can show up to others and offer real help.

This sixth house pokes holes in your confidence, not to tear you down but to make you better, much like the Virgo energy. This section helps you become more dedicated and aware of your responsibilities. It also shows the nature of your service and the people who serve you. Depending on the planet placements, you can understand more about this part if you have any there.

If you want to learn more about where you stand in the workplace and the nature of your relationship with your bosses, then the sixth house is the perfect section to check. You can see if you'll have power struggles, if your superiors will abuse your time and energy, or if you have an in with them. For instance, Mars in the sixth house can give you enough energy to work, but it can also cause tension with your colleagues because it will make you a bit competitive. A Scorpio placement might cause a chaotic environment between you and your colleagues.

That is not all that there is to the sixth house, though. It also rules your pets, whether they are yours or ones that live around you. You can love your pet all you want, but love is not enough to sustain its life. This is why the sixth house represents pets. You take care of them, and they give you love and affection in return.

This section also represents your health and well-being. You can learn more about the nature of your health through the sixth house sign and planet placements in this section. Generally, you want to see planets that will increase your vitality or provide you with good luck when it comes to your health.

Keyword: Duty
Planet Ruler: Mercury
Sign: Virgo

The Seventh House: The House of Relationships

The seventh house is ruled by Venus, the planet of love and beauty, and Libra, a social-centric sign that loves to love. The seventh house is where your intimate relationships are reflected. These relationships are represented by the seventh house sign and any planet placement in this section of your birth chart.

These kinds of relationships are not the only thing represented by this house. Your attitude towards them and the type of people you attract and are attracted to also occur in the seventh house. You can learn a lot about your attitude towards intimacy and your behavior around your partners. If you do not have any planets in that house and you want to learn more about your love language and how you love, you can study your Venus placement and aspects.

The seventh house is also home to the descendant, or DC for short. The descendant is opposite the ascendant, representing the first layer of your personality, or rather how people perceive you. The descendant is the exact opposite, as it represents a deep part of you that not everyone gets to see. Some astrologists think the descendant's traits are suppressed qualities within you. Others believe that the qualities of the DC are what you seek in other people, namely partners.

The two schools of thought could apply on so many levels that you can interpret your DC either way. Some astrologists think that the DC sign can show you the qualities you look for in a partner, or rather the qualities to which you are attracted.

Astrologists also believe that the seventh house does not just represent intimate relationships. It shows your close friendships or partnerships in general. So, your best friend, a close business partner, or a life partner is represented by your seventh house placements.

Note that the sign of your DC does not necessarily imply that your life partner's sun sign will be the same sign as your DC's. However, it could indicate the kind of qualities that they embody. For instance, if you have a Cancer DC, you may be attracted to loving and nurturing partners.

Perhaps you want someone to take care of you for a change or someone who makes you feel at home. Others with Capricorn DC might be attracted to partners who will help them get their life together and their tasks in order. Maybe they are attracted to someone who is financially well-off and budget-conscious.

Placements in the seventh house are extremely important because they heavily impact your relationships in life. For example, someone with Uranus placement in the seventh house might be attracted to eccentric and freedom-loving people. However, this placement also suggests that their relationships might end abruptly or without a specific reason. Another interpretation is that the individual might experience unstable relationships or that they attract unstable relationships that end up causing chaos in their wake.

Keyword: Cooperation

Planet Ruler: Venus

Sign: Libra

The Eighth House: The House of Death

The eighth house is ruled by Pluto, the planet of death and rebirth, and Scorpio, the secretive and intense sign. The eighth house is linked to various aspects, but they are all related to Plutonian themes.

The eighth house comes after the seventh, the house of partnerships. This section of your natal chart tells you the story of the happily ever after. It tells you what your life will be like after you have shared or merged your life with another. It answers questions like, how smooth is the merge going to be? Will one partner control the other? What will life look like after the union?

Through merging your life with your partner's, emerges a new you. Sharing your energy, time, and personal assets puts you in various situations with your partner that change both of you. Through this, the old you die, and the new self is rebirthed, which makes sense since Pluto rules this house. However, you and your partner will experience some friction and tension because controlling Scorpio will try to have the upper hand. However, there is no upper hand in healthy relationships, and that is what you come to learn through time and emotional growth.

Planet placements in this house are highly important too. One planet can make the eighth house themes easy for you, while others can cause slowness, anger, or frustration. Neptune placement can cause a lack of boundaries in the relationship and illusions about who your partner is. It can also cause an individual to be delusional regarding the relationship's flaws or major relationship problems. Ideas about sex and transformation of identity can be weakened with that placement, so the individual has to go through a process of metamorphosis to wake up and be disillusioned from Neptune's blindness.

The eighth house allows us to resolve the events that occurred in the fourth house. The fourth house mainly resembles the mother, so if your relationship with her was turbulent or void of love, these themes are bound to reoccur in the eighth house, and it puts you at risk of losing your relationship with your partner. The individual has to go through a process of facing ancient fears regarding losing someone they love or losing someone who loves them. This can only result in one of two ways, succumbing to these fears or healing from them. Either way, Pluto will ensure that the individual is completely transformed during this phase of their lives.

The eighth house also has to do with inheritance, whether money or assets. For instance, Jupiter in this placement can influence many riches coming your way through inheritance. It can also help with tax inspectors and debt in general, unlike Saturn's influence, which can cause bankruptcy or having a partner who is not financially well off.

Keyword: Transformation
Planet Ruler: Pluto
Sign: Scorpio

The Ninth House: The House of Philosophy

Ruled by Jupiter, the planet of abundance and the higher mind, and Sagittarius, the philosopher, the ninth house is where you transcend in your natal chart. The ninth house is where you ask questions about existence and the meaning of life. As the 3rd house, the ninth house is mainly about thinking. However, the 3rd house is more concerned with facts, while the ninth house is concerned with abstract ideas.

To further elaborate, the ninth house is all about the higher mind. You might understand things in the third house, but you formulate a final opinion about them in the ninth.

This section is about seeking meaning. The ninth house fuels the need to understand the meaning behind life's struggles, why you are here, and other existential questions.

This is why this part is connected to God, or rather the idea of God and religion in general. It does not have much to do with faith, as much as it has to do with seeking knowledge of the things beyond our comprehension as human beings.

The ninth house can also reveal what kind of God you would pray to or which religion you would follow. It can also show you the nature of your spirituality. Maybe you are a person who does not believe in a higher power. Or maybe you do, but you do not necessarily want to follow a specific faith. If these areas are a mystery to you, perhaps it is time that you check your ninth house placements.

This part also has to do with traveling, foreign cultures, and individuals. The connection here is simple. As you elevate your mind and access your higher mind, you can elevate physically and enter a whole new world with different rules and norms than yours.

Traveling here works on two levels, both literally and figuratively. A Jupiter placement here can make you travel to many places, but it can also put you in situations where you travel with your mind or spirit. This could happen through meditation or any form of a spiritual experience.

The ninth house is about curiosity and mental stimuli. Any planet placement here is important. For instance, if you have Mars in the ninth house, you are straightforward with your communication, especially in disagreements. It also means that you need to be mentally stimulated in your daily life. Otherwise, boredom takes over.

If you have Venus in this area, then this means that you are attracted to people who can speak about the more abstract things in life with you. You are more likely to be interested in people who think philosophically and are not afraid to ask questions and examine the reality behind everything they have been taught.

Venus's placement here is rather optimistic. People with this placement believe that everything that happens to them is ultimately for the greater good. However, Saturn in the ninth house can make an individual have difficulty seeing the meaning behind life events. They can also believe that life is absurd and that there is nothing at work here.

Keyword: Ambition

Planet Ruler: Jupiter

Sign: Sagittarius

The Tenth House: The House of Social Status

The Medium Coeli, also referred to as Midheaven and MC, is located on the cusp of the 10th house. This is the epitome of your natal chart. Any planet placements stand out here in comparison to others. This is the energy you exude the most, people see you as this energy, and it is ideally how you would like to be seen.

For example, if you have Uranus in this position, then you might be inventive and original. People will pick up on that and see that you march to the beat of your own drum, and at the same time, you like that they view you as such.

To understand the MC, pay attention to its relationship with the IC. They are located opposite one another and reflect different sides or parts of your life. While the IC reflects your roots, home, unseen emotional life, energy, and past, the MC reflects the highest point you'll reach, career, seen energy, and future.

The tenth house is co-ruled by Saturn and Capricorn. Naturally, this house is associated with your career path along with discipline and dedication to achieving your professional desires. Sign and planet placements in this house can reveal the nature of your job and the approach you have regarding your career.

To further explain this, picture a Mars placement that shows that you will have a lot of drive and energy while pursuing your job or field. This placement can also show that you can be quite aggressive in your professional life.

If you have a Saturn placement here, you might be a stickler for the rules or do things by the book. It also suggests that you'll show up to work on time and have the qualities of an ideal employee. It could also show that you expect everybody to do the same in the workplace. People not sticking to the rules or doing things their own way can get on your nerves. You can have a limited view of how your employees or colleagues should complete tasks. Any alternative style that is different from yours will be considered inadequate or unprofessional.

Placements here can indicate the kind of energy you exude and that people pick up on. For instance, Cancer placements might present themselves as nurturing or caring, and people will view them as such. Neptune might be the dreamy, lost individual who is either the martyr or the victim of others.

If you are curious about your professional life and the energy you present to the world, you might want to study your placements in the tenth house. You can also check the aspects you have there, and if you do not have any, then check the sign that is on the cusp of your MC.

Keyword: Career

Planet Ruler: Saturn

Sign: Capricorn

The Eleventh House: The House of Friendships

The eleventh house is co-ruled by Saturn and Uranus. This makes this section of the birth chart fixated on relationships beyond us. This area reflects your community, whether it is a religious, spiritual, political, or social group. This section also reflects our dynamic in said community. It shows which part we naturally play and can reveal the people or communities to which we are attracted.

According to astrologists, the effects of Saturn and Uranus give different tones to this house. The interesting factor here is that both planets add different energies that may clash sometimes. For instance, Saturn may want exclusion. It is not comfortable with new members in the group nor changes in the group dynamic. On the other hand, Uranus is open to everyone and is comfortable with trying new things or shifting from the old ways to the new.

Saturn in the eleventh house may be overly concerned with groups different from it. For instance, Saturn here might be worried about immigrants in its country or the new neighbors in its town. Check if you have this planet there and study its placements. Remember that it will only inspire worry in you. However, you can still come around to the diverse group you are surrounded by, channeling more Uranus and Aquarius energy associated with this house.

This house prioritizes humanitarian causes and innovation and is highly affected by Aquarius energy. This sign is mainly fixated on justice for humanity, harmony, balance between all social groups, openness and willingness to shed away the old ways, and readiness for a better tomorrow.

To know more about where you stand in all of this, check the kinds of placements you have. Study your eleventh house sign and the planets with their aspects, if you have any there. Here is how you can interpret your placements. If you have the moon there, you might be most comfortable with people similar to you. Similar here means that you share the same beliefs and philosophies. You will also be emotionally connected to the causes you are involved in.

A Venus placement here can work on two levels. Regarding your social life, Venus will give you social intelligence; you'll be the furthest thing from being socially inept. You will appreciate being in a group dynamic, and people will naturally gravitate toward you. Relationship-wise, you can learn about the kind of relationships you like to be in. Venus here may be attracted to originality and eccentricity, mirroring Aquarius energy.

Remember that any planet can be afflicted, so your Venusian energy in the eleventh house can affect you in both beneficial and disadvantageous ways. Check the aspects that Venus has here with other planets. If you do not have hard aspects, you can consider this placement beneficial.

Keyword: Social Awareness

Planet Co-Rulers: Uranus and Saturn

Sign: Aquarius

The Twelfth House: The House of Endings

The twelfth house is one of the deepest and most mysterious houses on the birth chart. This section rules the unknown as a concept, such as anything that is secretive or has been locked away in your brain or things that are beneath the surface. This includes things like your hidden weaknesses and strengths. As Neptune and Pisces also rule your subconscious, it is also ruled by this house. Your subconscious is powerful, especially since it has stored information that you have long forgotten about ever since birth. You act based on what your subconscious thinks is safe, and so you often get yourself in trouble in friendships and relationships.

The great thing about this house is that it gives you clues and reveals what goes on in your subconscious. Studying this part of your birth chart can help you with psychological issues of which you are unaware. If you have any planet placements in this house, then you must study its aspects. Twelfth house aspects can reveal so much about your subconscious thoughts, and you can begin your healing journey from there.

The twelfth house is also known as the house of karma. This is where your karma debt is stored. Once your karmic debt is revealed, you can learn about your past life experience and the kind of debts you need to clear during this lifetime.

When astrologists talk about the twelfth house, they always mention the concept of oneness. This is where your ego dies, and you become one with the whole again. For instance, if you have a Mercury placement, you might act like a mouthpiece for your community. You either speak for them or guide them in some way. If you have a Mars placement, you might be fighting your people's battles, expressing their fury, or acting upon it.

You can also link your twelfth house sign and planet and interpret them together to better understand. For instance, if you have a Libra and Mars, then you'll be fighting for justice. If you have Libra and Mercury, you'll speak for justice.

This section of your birth chart also resembles institutions in the background, such as hospitals and prisons. Institutions that keep people away from the rest of society. The twelfth house deals with secretive and underground issues, so naturally, it rules places that separate people from the community.

Not everyone has planets in their twelfth sign, so do not be alarmed if you do not have any. To better understand your twelfth house in terms of your subconscious and other related themes, check your Neptune and Pisces placements in your chart. Also, check the sign that is on the cusp of your twelfth sign and interpret it to understand more about the hidden parts of yourself.

Keyword: Subconscious

Planet Ruler: Neptune

Sign: Pisces

Chapter 5: The Major Planetary Aspects

A natal chart is a circle divided into twelve houses and twelve planets. The planets take up space according to the time of birth. There are two luminary bodies, eight major planets, and one minor planet distributed among the twelve sections of your birth chart. So that makes up eleven bodies around each other in one circle. With this kind of distribution, the bodies are bound to create angles, which is what Astrologists call aspects.

There are five major aspects divided into two categories, soft and hard aspects. Conjunction, sextile, and trine are considered to be soft aspects, while square and opposition are known as the hard aspects.

At the end of each aspect, you'll find an exercise that is designed to test your knowledge and how well you understand the function of each aspect.

Conjunction ♂

Conjunction happens when two planets are eight degrees apart. This is considered to be one of the strongest aspects of Astrology. When two planets are in such close proximity, their powers are blended, and they create a hybrid of sorts. They also heighten each other's influence, especially if their powers are harmonious.

For instance, if you have a conjunction between the moon and Venus, as both of these bodies are concentrated with feminine energy, this will result in high feminine power. You can expect harmonious emotions, powerful love for beauty, and a high intuition of this aspect.

Muhammed Ali has Mars in conjunction with MC. Based on this aspect, Ali had a powerful drive and determination to do everything in his own style. He also strongly identified with his goals and got angry and frustrated when someone tried to stop him.

Exercise:

State the aspect's degree and its influence:

1. The sun conjunct Jupiter.
2. Mercury conjuncts Mars.

Sextile ✳

Another soft aspect is a sextile. Traditional astrologists say that a sextile occurs when two planets are 60 degrees apart. Other Astrologists add or subtract 3 degrees from the original 60. Either way is correct.

A sextile is a strong harmonious aspect. Harmonious aspects usually take away the harsher qualities in a planet and combine the positive traits.

To understand this better, imagine that your Venus is in Sextile Mercury. This means that you have brilliant social skills and love harmony and balance within group dynamics. It also means that you are charming and know how to talk yourself out of unpleasant situations.

Take Nina Simone, for example. Her Venus is in sextile with Uranus. This means that she enjoyed spontaneous relationships that were built upon creativity. Based on Uranus's effect, her relationships might have been perceived as weird or different, but Miss Simone did not care about this.

Exercise:

State the aspect's degree and its influence:

1. Moon sextile sun.
2. Neptune sextile AC.

Trine △

Trine is the last soft aspect that evokes a harmonious relationship between planets. This aspect occurs when two planets are 120 degrees apart. Some astrologists are rigid with that degree, while others add or subtract 6 degrees from it and still consider it a trine.

For example, somebody with the sun in trine with Saturn is a person whose identity is based on being responsible, dedicated, and reliable. They are also loyal and generous in relationships, and they expect the same qualities in return. This aspect also suggests that this person's father taught them about taking accountability and the importance of being responsible.

Now, what happened here? The trine canceled the sun's self-centered traits and Saturn's harsh lessons and integrated the more positive characteristics of the two bodies, creating a soft aspect.

Another excellent example of this is Freddy Mercury, whose moon is in trine with Mercury. Mercury had a soothing voice that people loved listening to based on this aspect. He also needed an eccentric partner who could stimulate his mind with authentic communication.

Exercise:
State the aspect's degree and its influence:

1. Mars trine Jupiter.
2. Sun trine Uranus.

Square □

A square is a harsh aspect, and it occurs when there are 90 degrees between two planets. This aspect creates tension and brings about challenges that the person must face.

Depending on the planet's placements and which two square together, these challenges could be internal or external, or even sometimes both.

To better grasp this aspect, picture someone with the moon square mercury. This person will have a rough time expressing themselves emotionally. They might be inarticulate or feel like they cannot talk about their emotions at first. Now, this challenge is primarily internal. Although, gradually, it will create tension between them and their loved ones because the people around this person will feel shut out or that they are not trusted enough.

Ted Bundy's chart shows Pluto in Leo square Venus and Mercury in Scorpio. This implies that his relationships carried heavy Plutonian energy and that his mind and speech were strongly affected by Pluto's malefic influence. Pluto here brings about death, both literally and figuratively, and promotes secrecy and lying.

Exercise:

State the aspect's degree and its influence:

1. Sun square, Neptune.
2. Mars square IC.

Opposition ☍

Opposition is also considered a hard aspect as it occurs when the planets are 180 degrees apart. This aspect creates polarity, which causes disappointments, tension, and frustration.

For example, Mars, in opposition to Venus, creates a passionate love life with amazing sex, but it also causes intense relationships and stormy fights. This type of dramatic love can exhaust the person eventually, and they will have to deal with the violent turbulence in their love lives.

Diana, Princess of Wales, has Mars opposing the moon. This means that her internal emotions were at a constant polarity with her drive. She would often set aside her feelings to protect the people she loved or to complete her goals. She also had a great need to create a safe space for herself because she felt deeply vulnerable and emotionally unprotected.

Exercise:

State the aspect's degree and its influence:

1. Mercury opposite Neptune.
2. Venus opposite Pluto.

Chapter 6: Understanding Astrological Progressions

The regular natal chart describes your personality and the circumstances you were born. It explains why you behave and think in the way you do. It tells you in which areas you excel and the parts that need inner self-work. It shows you everything you were born with and how your childhood affected you and affected the molding of your personality.

This type of birth chart is not designed to show you how you have progressed or keep track of your growth. You need a different kind of chart for that, and fortunately, there is one. This kind of natal chart is called a "Progression chart," designed to inform you of your personal development and how your mind, personality, and life circumstances will morph over the years.

The progression chart is divided into secondary progression and Solar Arc Direction. The secondary progression is when the day becomes a year in the chart. This means that one degree will resemble one day that lasts for a year. Astrologists use this type of chart to see deeper into the movement of planets and understand how it is affecting you today.

One degree resembles one year in the Solar Arc chart instead of a day. Through this chart, you can see the changes within the next 30 years or more. You can see how the planets move and the kind of effects you'll experience based on their placements and the aspects they create.

Even though both charts are calculated differently and used for various purposes, the planets' movements are calculated in the same way. In the traditional birth chart, the Moon takes 27 ½ days to complete its trip around the chart. However, in a progressed chart, the Moon will take 27 ½ years to complete a full trip.

In this chapter, the planets are divided into two sections: the Inner and Outer planets. Inner planets move relatively more quickly than the outer ones. You are more likely to experience an inner planet progression in your life than an outer planet progression.

Inner Planets

The Sun

The sun takes 365 days to complete a full trip, which means that it spends 30 days in one sign. However, in a progressed chart, the Sun takes 30 years to move from one sign to the other. Imagine that the average life expectancy of humans is around 90 years. This means that people will experience three different Sun signs throughout their lives. So, what does this mean? This breaks the narrative that your zodiac sign is stagnant and will never change. People develop, grow, and change – and these kinds of transformations are reflected when the Sun, identity, and ego enter a new sign. However, you never really lose your natal Sun's traits, but you gain different identity traits when your progressed Sun has entered a new sign.

The Moon

A progressed moon will affect the sign's emotional environment.
Gregory H. Revera, CC BY-SA 3.0 <https://creativecommons.org/licenses/by-sa/3.0>, via Wikimedia Commons https://commons.wikimedia.org/wiki/File:FullMoon2010.jpg.

The progressed Moon will spend 2 ½ years in one sign. During these years, your internal emotional environment will be affected by the sign that it is in. Astrologers suggest that it would be better if people kept track of their progressed Moon and how it reacts with their natal Moon. It would also be best to check where the Moon falls and exalts because this will have a huge impact on your emotions. If there is a period where you find it hard to feel your feelings or are generally not in tune with your emotions, you might want to check if the Moon is in Scorpio since when the Moon falls in that sign, it does not function as well as it should.

Mercury

Progressed Mercury is often challenging to calculate since it goes through retrograde three or four times a year. So, it is not easy to track how many years it stays in one sign. This planet is infamous for its frequent retrograde, a phenomenon where the planet moves backward. This is somewhat disastrous because it has incredible power that affects communication, transportation, and anything technology-related.

To take precautions, people generally brace themselves before a Mercury retrograde, so they're vigilant when it comes to working, emails, and cars. Of course, if you suffer from the occasional bout of "foggy brain," this could be the retrograde's doing.

As a result of Mercury's retrograde, its transiting time is affected, and it can spend between 14 to 60 days in one sign. That may seem a bit unpredictable. However, you can always count on the fact that it will never be more than two signs away from the sun.

Based on this, you might want to check if your Progressed Mercury has moved every year. When it does, you'll be astrologically receiving a new brain. You will find that you think differently, have a new perspective on life, and have a different way of communicating.

Venus

Progressed Venus will change your social life a bit. If you are used to a particular group dynamic or have a specific socializing method, you can expect it to change when your Venus is in progression.

Picture a Gemini Venus progressing into Cancer. Progressed Venus in Cancer will make the individual feel tired from socializing as a Gemini does, and they need more alone time. This does not mean that they will become introverts. However, they will be more comfortable spending time with themselves, and they need it more than anything. In terms of their love life, they will feel they are more caring and nurturing, and maybe they will fall for someone with Cancerian characteristics.

Regarding Venus' retrograde, it moves backward for 42 days. Once you are conscious of Venus' effect on your life, you will automatically notice when it is in retrograde, which usually happens every 18 months. During this time of year, our relationship with money changes. We either reevaluate how we use it or spend it without caution.

You might find old lovers coming back into the picture again. You also might notice a sudden urge to text an ex or check upon them. This is not necessarily a bad thing. However, be aware that making emotional decisions during a Venus retrograde can be foggy and might get you into trouble later.

Mars

Depending on the placement, progressed Mars promises new opportunities and beginnings. During the new era of your Mars, you could feel new energy surging within you. Let us say that your Mars is in the last degree in Cancer and heading to Leo. Once it moves there, you'll be more energized and feel you can accomplish more than when the planet was in Cancer. Your sex life also may be affected by this transition. There is no telling what it will be like, so check the placement and the aspects that it has with your natal Mars.

The planet retrogrades every 26 months. During this time, people usually feel dull and can repress anger. Usually, motivation is low, and it is as if one lacks the energy and interest to do anything.

Outer Planets

Jupiter

Progressed Jupiter may give you a batch of new luck in a new area of life. It will expand whichever sign and house to which it has traveled. Let us say that your natal Jupiter is in the last degrees of the sixth house, and your progressed Jupiter is heading for the seventh. Your luck will shift from being work-centered to relationships and partnerships. That being said, you'll have better luck regarding your relationships. The only thing you might want to watch for is this planet's indulgence. Jupiter maximizes any house and signs it is in and retrogrades once every year. So, you might feel the urge to over-indulge yourself.

The effects of retrograde revolve around forceful behavior and unrewarded endeavors. You might feel like your efforts did not pay off, or you have been experiencing an unlucky streak for a while. You may experience difficulties traveling, spiritual lulls, and might feel that you cannot learn anything new.

Unfortunately, some people find that their bodies are afflicted during this phase. Jupiter rules thighs, blood, arteries, feet, and hips. This is not to say that the body will suffer during every retrograde. This will only happen if Jupiter's retrograde is mixed with a harsh aspect that may cause pain or discomfort in the previously mentioned body parts.

The good news is that Jupiter takes around four months to go back to its normal movement. So, while the effects may be somewhat annoying, it is helpful to remember that this stage is only temporary.

Saturn

Progressed Saturn is another slow-moving planet that may or may not move in your chart. However, if it does, you will experience new life lessons. These lessons might come from unprecedented restrictions in one of your life areas, but Saturn always has a reason. If this planet does move, you must pay attention to what Saturn is trying to teach you. The effects may not be pleasant, but they are necessary, and once you have learned your lessons, you'll barely feel the effects anymore.

For example, Progressed Saturn moves from fiery Aries to earthy Taurus. You will find that you are no longer being put in situations where you need to keep your cool, but you'll start having financial issues. These issues are about feeling financially insecure during this phase.

When Saturn takes something from you or puts you in difficult situations, it is trying to teach you how to create these things for yourself or achieve self-mastery so that life is not as challenging as it used to be.

This planet is also known as the "planet of Karma," so it is considered your karma rebalancing when it retrogrades. This could be for better or worse. It is completely up to you. During this phase, you might experience anxiety about changing career paths, financial security, and responsibilities. You might also find yourself reflecting on your relationships. The effects of retrograde cannot be generalized because it depends on which planet and house it is in.

Uranus

Progressed Uranus might bring sudden changes in your life and close certain chapters. This might happen suddenly, and it might alarm you at first, but Uranus brings about change whether it is convenient or not. Uranus moves very slowly, so there is nothing to worry about if you hate change. However, if this planet is in the final degrees of a sign, then you might want to keep an eye out. For instance, if Uranus is leaving Gemini and entering Cancer, you might leave your house, travel, or be away from your home, whether people or the physical place itself.

It retrogrades once every year, and this phase lasts approximately five months. You might experience the sudden urge to break free from whatever keeps you in place during this time. You might feel like you want to get rid of anything causing unhappiness. If you feel trapped in a relationship, cannot communicate with your family, or cannot stand your work, you might leave them during a retrograde. You also might feel extra rebellious and will want to speak against injustices or revolt against some kind of system.

Neptune

Progressed Neptune might cloud your judgment or memory based on its location. If Neptune is in Pisces or Cancer, it might make you want to be close to the water. You also might reveal things in your subconscious, or you might suddenly remember things that were long forgotten. With this planet, you might want to check your aspects because Neptune is tricky and can influence this phase in your life in a whole new direction.

Neptune retrogrades once every year and lasts for five or six months. It is fairly common for people to experience disillusionment during a Neptune retrograde. The fog that has been inhabiting your mind and eyes will finally be removed, and you'll be able to see things for what they truly are. This is where you can experience an awakening, or you might find out something that will cause you pain. However, regardless of your situation, try to remember that it is better to know the truth than to be comforted by deceit.

Pluto

Progressed Pluto is a bit dangerous. This planet is all about transformation. However, Pluto's transformation comes after going through a challenging time. The themes that follow this planet are power dynamics, sex, subconsciousness, death, rebirth, and regeneration. So, when this planet enters a different sign, you can anticipate what kind of transformations you are going through. You can foresee the problematic situations in which you might end up. Remember to check your Progressed Pluto aspects with the other planets.

Picture your Progressed Pluto leaving Leo and entering Virgo to understand this more. This tells you that everything surrounding your work ethic, career, service, and how you help others is about to change. You can tell if it is for the better or worse by checking its aspects with your natal planets, transits, and other progressed planets.

Pluto retrogrades for five months once a year. During this time, people go through difficult emotions. It will feel like there is a lot to uncover, especially if things have been kept in the dark. The retrograde exposes secrets, heightens difficult emotions, and highlights problematic areas in an individual's life.

Chiron

Chiron is another slow-moving minor planet, which means that it will take many years to cross over to another sign. However, if your Chiron is in the 29th degree, it will not take long until it moves to another sign.

Progressed Chiron gives you a new way to heal your wounds. It can light a new path that you have never explored. It can also expose a different wound of which you were not aware.

Chiron retrogrades for four to five months annually. Chiron's retrograde brings introspection, isolation, and self-reflection with it. It is now that it wants to isolate you, but it gives you much-needed time to be with yourself and tends to your emotional needs.

Chapter 7: Outer Planet Transits

Planets move at different speeds, some orbit around the sun faster than others. In Astrology, the planets are divided into two sections according to their pace. In this chapter, you'll learn about the outer planets. These planets have obtained this label because of their significantly slower pace.

You might be thinking, why should you care about the planet's speed if they do not change their placements in natal charts?

You are right; your planets do not change placements in your birth chart. However, when you check your transits, you'll find that they constantly change signs, houses, and aspects.

When you are checking your transits, you see the planets move in real life and how they interact with your natal planets. These transits affect your day-to-day life; they can influence your mood and your experience of certain life events.

Jupiter

Transiting Jupiter spends approximately 1 year in one sign, meaning that it takes 12 years to return to its natal placement. Traveling through the signs, this planet is bound to create some aspects. These aspects usually last about three weeks or so.

Jupiter is known to bring good fortune, so people usually expect exciting life events during its stay in any of the signs. This planet promises expansion, new opportunities, and travel experiences. The fortunes you'll be blessed with may differ every time because of the different signs and houses it will land in. Usually, this planet brings about fortunate events, but that is not always the case.

Various factors dictate what Jupiter is going to bring you. It is not as simple as studying its influence under one of the signs. You also need to be looking at the sign, house, aspects of natal and transit planets, and the transit's nature. Some transits are just transits, plain and simple. But sometimes, the transit is a Jupiter return or a retrograde even.

A Jupiter retrograde is when the planet moves backward every nine months and stays in this phase for four months. A Jupiter return is when the planet returns to its natal placement. When you experience this phenomenon, you can prepare yourself for a new adventure. This placement means that you are about to embark on a new chapter in your life. Jupiter will turn the page for you, and as it creates aspects such as square and opposition, it will bring about some challenges. These challenges are designed so you can grow and become the person that Jupiter has been manifesting.

Saturn

It takes Saturn 29.5 years to return to its original placement, which means that it spends two-and-a-half years in one sign. This planet is significantly heavy, so you are bound to feel its influence whenever it moves.

There are telltale signs whenever the planet transits to a different sign. You might be exhausted or lack the energy to do anything. You might also feel like you are not emotionally reactive, nothing is exciting enough, or everything feels bland, especially if the planet has created aspects with other planets. Usually, these aspects, good or bad, last for six weeks. Of course, if these aspects are created with the sun or moon, they will not last that long.

Understanding what Saturn wants from you helps you live through difficulties. This planet wants responsibility, dedication, and a sense of seriousness towards yourself, your career, your relationships, and your life path.

You could feel exceptionally frustrated, drained, and tired during these transits. One of the things that might help you is knowing the planet is trying to create the atrocities that will force you to get the hang of your life.

There is a common misconception that Saturn is only concerned with one's professional life, but that could not be farther from the truth. Your natal Saturn will reveal with what it is most concerned. Understanding that will help you understand the planet's transits and the aspects it creates. Eventually, you'll understand what is being asked of you and where you should channel your energy.

Answering Saturn's calls is highly important because every Saturn return will test you. As mentioned before, Saturn's return occurs every 3 years. So, complying with your Saturn's calls will help you immensely when Saturn returns to its natal position.

Uranus

When transiting, the planet stays in one sign for about 7 years. Uranus is one of the strongest planets, so strong that it can shake your entire life. It is not unusual for this planet's transits to completely disorient you and disorganize your life.

You can never misinterpret Uranian transits. Every time it travels to a different sign, you might feel like you have a deep urge to get out of certain situations, be someone different, or just rebel. This might create some tension and frustration within you, do not fight it or ignore it.

When you experience a Uranian transit, you are being asked to change. However, sometimes the planet does not wait until you make a move and forces you into the situation. This is where you are asked to improvise and make the best of the situation.

Uranian-themed situations are not always easy or fun to deal with, but they create an environment where you can finally shine. These situations might feel like they came out of nowhere or don't suit you, but that could not be farther from the truth.

This planet represents the side of you that wants to break out from tradition, aches for freedom, and strives for innovation. You have a rebellious side that Uranus will shine a light on. Even if you think you do not have these qualities within you, you do, but Uranian aspects and transits might only activate them.

Speaking of aspects, this planet's aspects are effective for three months and lessens after that period is over. Uranus creates an opposition around the age of 42. This is usually the "mid-life crisis" phase that humans go through. If you want to know more about this, check your Uranus transits by the time you are 42 and check your opposition aspect.

Through this transit, you can learn more about your mid-life crisis and what it will look like. What will you be breaking away from, and in which ways? It is normal to anticipate this period, so consulting your natal chart can ease your worries.

Another thing to note is that the planet does not want to break apart your life for no reason. You are meant to go through this experience to grow fully.

Neptune

Neptune changes signs every 14 years, and the kind of aspects that it creates last about two years. Neptunian transits can feel like a wave just hit you, or it can be very subtle. If you are going through a strong transit, who you are – and your life – might change drastically.

This planet is strongly tied to spiritual awareness and experiences. Some people start questioning their beliefs and are left in limbo. They are no longer sure what or who to believe in, and it feels like the unshakable just got away from them.

Others experience spiritual awakening for the first time in their lives. They start viewing their place in the world differently and seeing everybody and everything in a completely different light.

Another thing that you might experience during this phase is disorientation. You might be a bit forgetful and lost during this time. You will enter a room and forget what you came here for, misplace items, and forget where you last saw them. You also might be lost in the figurative sense, like lost in life, and cannot seem to find your direction or the path you are supposed to be on.

You may want to cope by escaping from your life during this time. You could be spending most of your time watching TV shows, getting distracted by others' lives, or whatever escapism looks like to you. Your physical energy also might be low during this time. Getting up and showing up for your work, tasks, and chores might feel more challenging, and getting out of bed alone will be an accomplishment.

However, you will not feel like this all the time. It might hit you when Neptune is entering or exiting a sign. Another thing to pay attention to is the aspects that the planet might make. Study them so that you know how to prepare yourself properly.

Pluto

Pluto is an exceptionally slow planet, so it can stay anywhere between 14 and 30 years under the same sign. It is also unclear how much Plutonian aspects last, but they do take a few years to lose their effect.

This planet is mainly known for having intense, transformative energy. Most astrologists paint Pluto in that light, but the toll of that transformation is not discussed as much as it should be.

Whenever this planet is in transit and travels to a different sign, your whole life almost falls apart because you need to change or grow more into the person you are meant to become. This could be a positive experience, but it is not easy. It is one of the heaviest experiences you could go through. Everything you have built and every idea you had about yourself falls to the ground. The planet is asking you to pick up the pieces and build your life from scratch because that is how it will make you grow.

This is quite frightening, and everyone has a different experience with this planet, so you can never know for sure what your experience will look like. To predict your Plutonian experience, check the sign and the house it will be in and study its aspects with natal and transit planets.

Astrologists explain that Pluto in transit goes through three stages. It starts with a feeling of general disturbance. It will seem like everything is working against you, or you cannot get anything right. This will be followed by a period of confusion. You will feel that you do not know what is causing this disruption, and you will not know how to fix it. The final stage is the new self. This new you will not always be a more mature person, but it can be anything depending on how you have handled this difficult situation.

Chapter 8: Inner Planet Transits

Now that you are familiar with outer planetary transits, it is time that you familiarize yourself with the inner transits.

Inner planets move at a much faster pace than outer planets. This is why most astrologers keep up with their movements more often than they check the outer planets.

Take luminary bodies, for instance. They move every day, which means that you are constantly affected by their ever-changing degrees and aspects. They affect your mood, perspective, and so much more.

The Sun

The sun moves one degree every day and lands in a new sign every month. The sun represents your ego, self-perception, and your identity. When your transit sun creates aspects with other planets, your sense of self is affected. Usually, these aspects last for a maximum of three days. Their effects are not strongly felt, but you can still feel them. These aspects are more subtle, and while they affect you, they can be easily shaken off.

If you want to keep up with your transit sun, you'll need to check it frequently throughout the week. You might think it is unnecessary since its influence is not that strong. You are right, and its aspects will not sweep the rug from underneath you like outer planets. However, it will be creating aspects left and right because of its fast pace. This means that you'll be dealing with different aspects daily.

Depending on its aspects, your transit sun might make you feel like you are not happy with your current state in life. Maybe your position professionally, the furniture in your house, car, face, body, relationships, etc. Anything connected with who you are as a person or reflects your ego might be in question with your transit sun.

This does not mean that you'll be in a constant state of dissatisfaction with yourself and your life, but these are just some of the things you might experience.

More aspects created by your transit sun will make you feel like you are on top of everything in life. So, it depends on the aspects; you can quickly check these now and again.

The Moon

The moon moves much faster than the sun, and it travels to a new sign within two to two-and-a-half days. This luminary body affects your emotions, and with its high speed, you can understand why your feelings are constantly changing.

The moon also represents your home, family, and community. It represents them in the literal and figurative sense. The moon's movements influence even the idea of a home or family. It also impacts your unconscious habits and the kind of decisions you take while you are on auto-pilot.

Your transit moon's aspects can affect you to certain degrees, depending on how strong they are. For instance, if you have been having a tough time emotionally getting up and doing something, a transit moon in Aries can help you. Aries is all about being proactive, so an Aries moon might help you with your demotivation or lack of energy.

Mercury

The planet of communication and intellectuality spends three weeks in each sign. So, you can also expect it to make plenty of aspects, but they will only last for two days or so.

One of the aspects that you might want to pay attention to is transit Mercury to natal Mercury. Some aspects can cloud your thinking, and others can elevate your mental faculties.

Transit mercury does not just affect your thinking; it can also influence your communication, writing, reading, and perception of the world. Some challenging aspects can slur your speech or make you inarticulate. These aspects usually go away in a few days. However, you do not want to start an argument, have a serious conversation, or sign contracts when going through a difficult Mercury aspect.

Other transits can entice your curiosity. You might be bookmarking intriguing articles, buying new books, and making conversations with everyone around you during this time.

It is fairly easy to keep track of this planet. All you need to do is check its sign, its house, and its aspects with the transit and natal planets.

Venus

The planet of love and pleasure spends around 18 days in a zodiac sign, and its aspects last for 2 days. Transiting Venus will affect your relationships, whether they are intimate or casual friendships. It will also affect your sense of pleasure, so one day, you might feel like you want to go to a fancy place and appreciate your surroundings. On other days, you might want to be immersed in a cozy hangout, sunken into the couch, eating takeout, and watching your favorite TV shows with your loved ones.

You do not need to check your Venus as often as luminary bodies. However, you might want to check the aspects that it creates. Especially if you feel like something is off with your love life and social life.

You also need to know how your transit Venus affects your natal Venus. Sometimes, your love life can feel weird with difficult aspects, like opposition or square. You might be too closed off or cold. You might feel like you cannot stand your partner, or maybe you are more prone to arguments.

Softer aspects, like the conjunction, trine, or sextile, can add a more harmonious feel to your relationship. You might want to pay attention to conjunction aspects because, for instance, your transit with Venus might conjunct with Pluto. In that case, your relationship might go through a heavy transitioning period.

Mars

Mars transits are tricky.
NASA Hubble, CC BY 2.0 <https://creativecommons.org/licenses/by/2.0>, via Wikimedia Commons, https://commons.wikimedia.org/wiki/File:A_Dust_Storm_on_Mars.jpg

Mars is the slowest of all the inner planets, so it stays in one sign for about two months, and its aspects last around a week.

Transiting Mars is tricky because it gives you energy, but it can make you short-tempered and somewhat feisty. For instance, if this planet is transiting your 3rd or 11th house, you might feel the urge to fight with your siblings since these houses represent them.

Mars has a similar effect when it creates an aspect with your natal sun. You can feel angrier than usual, and you are more prone to tantrums or initiating an aggressive argument.

When transiting Mars has softer aspects, it can feel like you have more energy. You might notice that you are more proactive and ready to initiate projects and finish them. You can also finish tasks in a short amount of time and have more energy to finish more.

You can also feel more masculine energy surging through you, so when you feel that, just understand that that is your transit Mars' doing. This planet also influences your sex life along with your libido. So, you might feel more active or inactive during this time, depending on the planet's aspects.

Chapter 9: Reading an Astrology Chart

Congratulations! You have made it this far. You know all about the zodiac signs, planets, houses, and aspects. You have a good understanding of the different energies that they carry, how they influence you, and how they create certain life events.

You will notice that the knowledge you have accumulated is taking effect once you try interpreting your natal chart. You might not know how to do this yet, but once you are done reading this chapter, you will start to understand how astrological interpretations work.

The Natal Chart

Sample natal chart.
https://commons.wikimedia.org/wiki/File:Goethe_Natal_Chart.png

You might not be accustomed to reading a natal chart yet, but you'll find that it is the best teacher even if you do not understand everything about it yet. This is why you might want to have your natal chart open as you read this chapter to better understand it.

Here are the steps that you should follow to get your birth chart. Go to astro.com. You will find a tab on the left next to the "Horoscopes" tab; click on it. Then click on "Free Horoscopes." Click on "Charts and Data." which will open another menu with different selections. In that selection, click on "Extended Chart Selection."

The website will take you to a new page with guest users and visitors. Click on "guest user" and fill in your information. You will find a pop-up tab asking you to put in your time of birth as you do so. You can ask anyone in the family if they know exactly when you were born. After you have that piece of info, go ahead, and fill it in.

The website will take you to a new page, scroll down and click on "Options for zodiac and houses." Find "House System" and click on "Placidus." Scroll down further and select "Display and calculation options," then click on "True Node" and "Descending Node." Scroll down again, find "Aspects," then click on "to Chiron" and "to all objects." Finally, select "Additional objects" and select "Lilith." After you are done, select "Click here to show the chart."

Reading the Natal Chart

Welcome to your birth chart! You will find a big circle that is divided into 12 houses. Inside these houses, you might find symbols for the planets. You can refer back to chapter 2 or go to the glossary to understand which planets correspond to which symbols. You will also notice the zodiac signs on the circumference of the circle.

As you may have noticed, every sign aligns with a certain house, and these houses may or may not contain any planets; this is normal. If you have three or more planets in the same house, this is called a "Stellium." It means that one of your houses is influenced by a number 0f planetary energies.

An easy way to read your chart is through a binary system. You will be reading the houses that are opposite one another, so you can quickly understand what each house represents and interpret it as you go along. Remember that all the houses have multiple meanings, so make sure you refer back to Chapter three to have a good grasp on the energies that each house contains.

Start with your ascendant, which is on the cusp of the first house. Opposite it, you'll find the descendant, which is on the cusp of the seventh house. The first house is the self, which automatically means that the seventh house is other people. If you have any planets in the first house, understand that they affect your self-perception. If you have planets in the seventh house, these energies affect your relationships with others, whether intimate relationships, friendships, or acquaintances.

Pay attention to your ascendant sign and learn more about the planet that rules it. For instance, if your AC is on the cusp of Taurus, then Venus has the rulership here. Why is this important?

In Astrology, the planet that rules the AC sign is also the planet that has rulership over your natal chart. This means that you are affected strongly by that specific planet, and you'll will feel your natal Venus' aspects heavily, whether they are good or bad. The same logic applies when the planet is in transit or retrograde.

You can then move on to the second house, which represents personal resources. Opposite the second house is the eighth house which represents shared resources. If you do not have any planets in the second house, do not worry. It does not mean that you do not have ownership over your money or that you'll be going through financial difficulties. If you want to better understand your finances through astrology, check the sign on the cusp of your second house, the tenth house, and Taurus and Venus since they are associated with money.

Now you can see that the third house, opposite the ninth house, is connected to your cognitive understanding and abstract thinking. Then you can move on to the fourth house and the tenth house, which represent your roots and destination in this life. You will also find the IC on the cusp of the first house and the MC on the cusp of the tenth house.

Now start looking at your fifth house, which represents your inner creativity, pleasure, and children. Opposite it, you'll find the eleventh house, which represents adopted children and your friendships and social life.

The last houses you'll look at now are the sixth and the twelfth. The sixth is about serving others, whether it is through our jobs or helping the general public. The twelfth is more behind the scenes and more connected to the subconscious and behind-the-scenes action.

Further Readings and General Notes

Reading a natal chart can be complicated at first, but the easier it becomes, the more you practice. Here are a few tips to help you get started.

You might find it significantly helpful to note down the areas of life represented by each house. You can go back to Chapter four and summarize each house. You can use keywords to help you with that. For instance, the 1st house is the house of the self. The second house is the house of personal resources and so on.

You can do the same thing with the zodiac signs and the planets. This will help you figure out your birth chart in such a short amount of time.

One of the things that might help with your interpretation is dedicating a few pages to each of the houses. Start with the first house, and write down its zodiac sign and the planets that this house contains. If there are planets in this house, then it is essential to know about their aspects in terms of other planets.

This can be a never-ending process because the more you learn, the more you'll find new things to note down. It is important to keep track of your notes and add to them every time you learn something new.

It is also vital that you keep track of your progress if you want to be an advanced astrologer because, eventually, you will see how far you have come compared to when you started this journey. This will help you gain confidence in your skills and increase your pace when interpreting anyone's natal chart.

You will find a certain zodiac sign on the cusp of each house. This zodiac sign tells you how you behave with the house's energy. For instance, let us say that you have had Virgo on the cusp of your eleventh house. This means that you like helping your friends, and in your friendships, your function as the helper and your friends depends on you when they need help. Another example is if you have Capricorn in your first house, this could mean that you are not comfortable sharing your vulnerable feelings, and you may have come out of a house that was often called and did not pay attention to you.

You will also find various lines in the center of your natal chart, the aspects discussed in chapter five. To check your aspects in-depth, select "Additional tables." You are going to see each aspect of all of the planets. Here is how you can read them. Picture a Mercury trine Venus aspect. This means that you are charming and have good social skills. It also means that you are good with communication and usually know what to say.

Another example would be a Mars square Saturn. This means that you probably grew up around a lot of criticism or endured strict discipline. This leads to problems with authentic self-expression and Saturn hindering the Mars energy in you. You might fear success and have difficulty chasing after what you need or desire.

Go back to the natal chart tab and select "+ With transits." This tab will show you all of your transit planets, where they stand, and their aspects with your natal planets. You can read these aspects by selecting "Additional tables," except you will have three tables. One is for your natal planets, another is for your transit planets, and the third is for the aspects between your natal and transit planets.

Remember that transits' effects do not last, so when studying the transits that you are or will be experiencing, make sure to write down their duration. Another thing that might help you with this is to journal how you feel during this transit.

Acknowledging your emotions during a smooth or rough transit can allow you to predict what a similar transit will be like in the future. Observe the life events you are experiencing through this transit and notice your emotional experience.

Here are some helpful questions to get you started. How do I feel during this transit? What kind of life events am I experiencing now? How am I reacting to these life events?

Make sure that you have the transiting planet at the top of the page, which sign and house it is transiting in, and the kind of aspects it has. Then write the duration of the transit and the duration of the aspects. This will give you a clearer picture of what you are dealing with and help you be emotionally prepared for similar transits.

Chapter 10: Solar and Lunar Returns

Solar Return

You have been unknowingly celebrating your solar return every year now. A solar return is when the sun returns to the exact position at the time of your birth.

The sun represents your ego and identity, and so with a solar return, it is as if you are being welcomed into a new you. You will not change overnight, but you can think of it as starting a new chapter.

You can quickly check your solar return by adding your location, time, and date of birth to a website that calculates it for you.

It is also best to see your whole solar return chart because it is a forecast for the entire year, at least until your next solar return. You will notice that all the planets are in different placements. The planets will be in different signs and houses, and even your ascendant will be different.

This chart can tell you the themes that you'll be experiencing during your new year. You must study these planets' placements and aspects and understand what they will mean for you. Try to interpret their locations as much as possible to prepare yourself for what is yet to come.

You can also learn a lot about how your identity will change throughout the year and the challenges you'll face.

Lunar Return

The lunar return is a cosmic phenomenon that you experience every month. As mentioned before, the moon moves at a relatively fast pace, so every month, it returns to the exact position of your natal moon. Let us say that you are a 26th-degree Libra moon. When you experience a lunar return, it means that currently, the transit Moon is in the same sign and degree as the moon phase under which you were born.

Astrologists claim that lunar returns give you the clarity to experience honest emotional self-reflection. They recommend journaling and going in-depth about how you have been feeling lately and connecting with yourself. Try to avoid running away from your emotions or unpleasant feelings during this time because even though they may be unpleasant, they still give you the reward of emotional clarity.

You can also look more into your unconscious habits. If you have been unhappy about your relationship with food and how you use your time, you can reflect on these topics during this time of the month.

After you have done yourself the service of self-reflection under the moon's influence, you might notice that you can make more conscious and healthier choices in your day-to-day life.

You can calculate your lunar return using Astro.com or other astrological apps and websites. You need to add the time and date of birth and the exact location where you were born. The website will show you the exact time of your lunar return and the kind of aspects you'll be experiencing then.

The Difference

The solar return is all about your identity and personality, while the lunar return is more emotionally oriented and more connected with your subconscious.

Now, take a look at your solar and lunar charts. You will notice that the planets are scattered differently around your natal chart, so what does that mean? How will these placements affect you during this year?

Solar return planets represent everything that has to do with your personality, so let us say that you have a Pluto in the seventh house in your solar return chart. This means that you'll be experiencing yourself through relationships with others. It could be through intimate relationships, friendships, acquaintances, etc. It also means that you will go through a transformative experience. The way you treat others may change, or you might take a good hard look at yourself and change the things you do not appreciate about how you interact with others.

The same logic can be applied to your lunar return chart. If you have Pluto in the sixth house, you might feel that you are wasting too much energy in your work or service to others, and it is time to shift that energy towards yourself. You will feel drained and need to give more love and attention to yourself.

A solar chart is like an annual forecast, while a lunar chart is a monthly forecast. You can study the kind of themes you'll be experiencing regarding your identity and emotionally through both of these charts.

Glossary of Glyphs

In this bonus chapter, you'll be able to find every glyph mentioned throughout this book. You can refer to this section when you are studying or interpreting your natal chart.

Aspects

Major Aspects

1. Conjunction: ☌

2. Trine: △

3. Sextile: ✳

4. Square: ☐

5. Opposition: ☍

Geometrical Points

1. Black Moon Lilith: ⚸

2. North Node: ☊

3. South Node: ☋

Luminary bodies

1. Sun: ☉

2. Moon: ☽

Planets

1. Mercury: ☿

2. Venus: ♀

3. Mars: ♂

4. Jupiter: ♃

5. Saturn: ♄

6. Uranus: ♅

7. Neptune: ♆

8. Pluto: ♇

9. Chiron: ⚷

Points in the Natal Chart

1. Ascendant: AC
2. Descendant: DC
3. Medium Coeli: MC
4. Imum Coeli: IC

Signs

1. Aries ♈

2. Taurus ♉

3. Gemini ♊

4. Cancer ♋

5. Leo ♌

6. Virgo ♍

7. Libra ♎

8. Scorpio ♏

9. Sagittarius ♐

10. Capricorn ♑

11. Aquarius ♒

12. Pisces ♓

Conclusion

Throughout the centuries, Astrology has been the central practice playing an important role in humanity's spirituality. The more humanity learned about it, the greater their understanding of it became. Humans did not stumble upon the art of predictive Astrology in one day, and it took centuries to develop this knowledge.

Predictive Astrology adds depth to your life. It is not just about knowing what might happen a week or month from now. It is more about the challenges you'll meet, the growth you'll experience, and reaching the purest version of yourself.

Through the knowledge of Astrology and Numerology, you learn more about your path in this lifetime. You understand what you need to overcome and adjust in your character or life to be on the path best suited for you. You gain perspective and reach a higher level of consciousness just by absorbing this kind of knowledge.

The energies that planetary bodies carry influence your life significantly, whether it is through life events, who you were born as, or the kind of home you grew up in. Everything that you experience in life is influenced by all the energies that are around you, including the power of numbers.

Numerology reveals the nature of the hidden energies that reside within you. These energies affect your traits and make up your unique personality. They are what makes you stand out and the reason behind your unexplained stamina, perseverance, or kindness. Numbers also carry energies that correspond with your life path, so once you figure out your path, the road ahead seems clearer, and you know where to head now.

The power of Astrology and Numerology is real, so use it wisely, whether to help yourself or a loved one. Remember that the more you practice reading natal charts, the easier it will become, so practice here is critical. Once you have mastered your skills, you will better understand how your life is influenced by the universe and work with it, not against it.

Here's another book by Mari Silva that you might like

Your Free Gift
(only available for a limited time)

Thanks for getting this book! If you want to learn more about various spirituality topics, then join Mari Silva's community and get a free guided meditation MP3 for awakening your third eye. This guided meditation mp3 is designed to open and strengthen ones third eye so you can experience a higher state of consciousness. Simply visit the link below the image to get started.

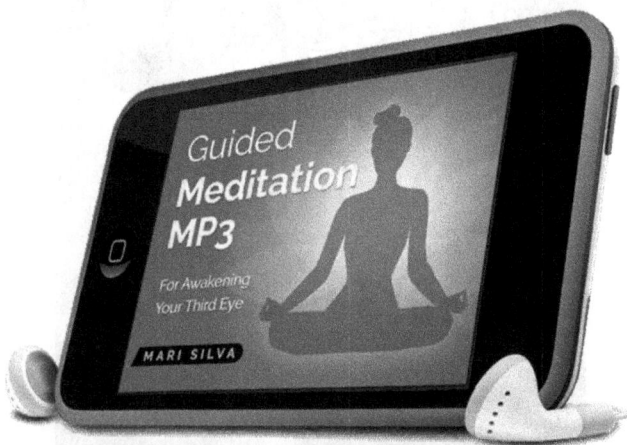

https://spiritualityspot.com/meditation

Resources

Buchanan, M. (2013). The Numerology Guidebook: Uncover Your Destiny and the Blueprint of Your Life. Hay House, Inc.

Dodge, E. (1988). Numerology has your number. Simon and Schuster.

Fanthorpe, L., Lionel, F., & Fanthorpe, P. (2013). Mysteries and secrets of numerology (Vol. 16). Dundurn.

Heyss, J. (2001). Initiation Into Numerology: A Practical Guide for Reading Your Own Numbers. Weiser Books.

Kapil, A. (2001). Numerology Made Easy. Penguin Books India.

Lagan, H. A. (2011). Chaldean Numerology for Beginners: How Your Name and Birthday Reveal Your True Nature & Life Path. Llewellyn Worldwide.

Lawrence, S. B. (2019). The Big Book of Numerology: The Hidden Meaning of Numbers and Letters. Weiser Books.

Mykian, W. (2011). Numerology Made Easy: An Introduction to the Chaldean Science of Numbers. Xlibris Corporation.

Ojha, P. A. (2005). Numerology for All. Orient Paperbacks.

Sharp, D. (2001). Simple Numerology: A Simple Wisdom Book. Conari Press.

Simpson, J. (2014). Numerology: Make Predictions and Decisions Based on the Power of Numbers. Penguin.

Singh, S. C. (2020). Let the Numbers Guide You: The Spiritual Science of Numerology. John Hunt Publishing.

Thompson, L. B. (1999). Chaldean Numerology: An Ancient Map for Modern Times. Tenacity Press.

Visconti, S. (2020). Numerology: Discover The Meaning Behind The Numbers in Your life & Their Secrets to Success, Wealth, Relationships, Fortune Telling

& Happiness. Sofia Visconti.

Windfuhr, G. (2004). Zoroastrian and Taoist Ritual: Cosmology and Sacred Numerology. In Zoroastrian Rituals in Context. Brill

Cunningham, D. (1993). Moon Signs: The Key to Your Inner Life. Ballantine Books.

G. (2014). Depth Astrology: An Astrological Handbook, Volume 3--Planets in Houses. Independently published.

Kent, E. A. (2015). Astrological Transits: The Beginner's Guide to Using Planetary Cycles to Plan and Predict Your Day, Week, Year (or Destiny). Fair Winds Press.

Ma, R. K. B. (2007). Llewellyn's Complete Book of Astrology: The Easy Way to Learn Astrology (Llewellyn's Complete Book Series, 1). Llewellyn Publications.

March, M. D., & McEvers, J. (2008). The Only Way to Learn Astrology, Volume 1, Second Edition (2nd ed.). ACS Publications.

McQuillar, T. L. (2021). Astrology for Mystics: Exploring the Occult Depths of the Water Houses in Your Natal Chart. Destiny Books.

Sasportas, H., & Greene, L. (2009). The Twelve Houses. LSA/Flare.

Sears, K. (2016). Astrology 101: From Sun Signs to Moon Signs, Your Guide to Astrology (Adams 101). Adams Media

www.ingramcontent.com/pod-product-compliance
Lightning Source LLC
Chambersburg PA
CBHW071857090426
42811CB00004B/649